To Lynn, Ally, James, and Mary

CHAPTER 1

It was the first COVID-19 summer. Masks were in use, and people were social distancing. Many people had died. A vaccine was hoped for by the end of the year. Variant mutations had not yet been imagined.

David Richards was sitting at a wrought iron table on his elevated porch in Elbert County, Colorado, approximately seven miles north of the rural town of Elizabeth. A set of eight steps consisting of thick flagstone slabs descended from his porch to a lower flagstone porch with a stone fireplace ring. The steps divided a retaining wall around the back of his house. On the right side of the steps were red-flowered butterfly bushes. Hummingbirds took turns dive-bombing their hummingbird competitors and drinking nectar from the long red blossoms. On the left side of the steps were yellow sunflowers. These blooms were being attended to by goldfinches with yellow bellies and olive-green heads and backs. The finches were so small that they could land on a sunflower without making the stalk bend.

There were Austrian pines in a semicircle behind the twenty-foot-diameter flagstone lower patio. Fifty yards beyond the patio to the west was a barn with a weather vane used to store yard and gardening equipment. Another fifty yards westward was David Richards's fence line. Beyond the fence line was a ranch that raised Herford and Texas longhorn cattle. The ranch was called Spring Valley Ranch. The ranch had a stream running through it and a thick line of ancient cottonwoods, some reaching two hundred feet tall.

It was late August, and the trees were magnificently green and lush. An occasional smattering of yellow leaves foretold the coming of fall. Spring Valley Ranch was 6,200 feet in elevation, so early snows often came in mid-September.

David was sipping a Dale's Pale Ale on his painted concrete back porch. There was a slight breeze that mitigated the August afternoon heat. David heard a low growl from his dog, Grady, who was sleeping underneath the table. Grady was looking out at the western fence line and could see that a red fox had jumped over the fence. Grady, a thin but sturdy mixture of German shepherd and Airedale, was accustomed to foxes and coyotes walking along the western fence line to tease him. His fur bristled, but Grady had long ago given up chasing his elusive wild cousins. He would occasionally bark but usually just growled his protective growl.

David reached down and scratched the ears of his eighty-pound canine friend. Glancing to the south, David could see the top of Pike's Peak in the clear air. It looked deceptively close even though the mountain was about one hundred miles away.

David often imagined that his property would have made an excellent campground for the Native Americans who once roamed this prairie. One could see enemies or game approaching from miles away. The stream running through Spring Valley was the only water source around. Kiowa and Comanche were the first known native tribes in the area. They were later displaced by the Cheyenne and Arapahoe. Unfortunately, David had yet to find any native artifacts that would support his theory.

This house was Jen's house. His late wife had searched the real estate market and looked at many properties before she chose this one. She had a residential real estate background and hired a local realtor to help her with the selection. She also had a grand plan for the landscaping and decoration. The house was a Mediterranean with a stucco and stone exterior. David had made a concerted effort to continue her landscaping plans and tend to her exterior foliage design. In fact, in the last two years, he had spent more time working outside than he ever had. He considered it a good therapy.

Jen had died two years ago. She'd been working in the southeast suburban Denver area marketing commercial office space. She rarely got home before dark. That fall night, it was cloudy and darker than usual. She was only two and a half miles from home when she reached the intersection of Singing Hills Road and Elbert County Road 13. Presumably, she stopped at the four-way stop sign.

As she accelerated to reach the 50 mph speed limit for Singing Hills Road, a mule deer doe darted out from the ditch, and she hit it with the full force of her Subaru Forester. The investigating sheriff's deputy, who was an accident reconstructionist for Elbert County, told him he could not be sure whether Jen died upon impact with the deer—as it came through the windshield—or whether she died upon making impact with a pine tree on the slope descending from Singing Hills Road. In either case, her demise would have been swift and probably painless. David never pursued any further reconstruction of the accident. What difference would it make?

Grady growled again, but his tail started wagging as he looked through the sliding glass door and into David's kitchen. A familiar face to both of them opened the sliding door and joined David at the wrought iron table and chairs. He was Marc Goodman, David's law partner. Of medium height, he had salt-and-pepper short hair and wore a lawyer's navy three-piece suit. Marc Goodman was the type of friend who had a key to David's house and never had to knock before entering. They had always been good friends, and remained so even after David started to plan his retirement.

David had kept working in his role as an active trial attorney for several months after Jen's death, but he seemed unfocused and eventually quit accepting new case assignments. Both David Richards and Marc Goodman had made a substantial amount of money as plaintiff's trial attorneys in their firm, Goodman and Richards, PC. They had a solid reputation for being willing to take cases to trial and getting successful results. Most of those results came in high-profile referrals for David to be the lead trial attorney. "High profile" meant a substantial likelihood of a large plaintiff's verdict in the personal injury industry.

Both Marc and David had spent their formative years in the Denver District Attorney's Office, where they learned their trial skills. Neither was afraid to take any meritorious case to a jury. In a plaintiff's personal injury practice, the ability to take cases to trial and win was essential. The insurance companies were risk-avoiders by their nature, and a reputation for high verdicts and the ability to take a case all the way to a verdict was an extremely valuable asset for a personal-injury attorney.

Both David Richards and Marc Goodman were at the zenith of their legal careers when David decided to slow down and quit taking new cases. Marc was a true friend of David's, as well as being his business partner. Marc had thought the best way for David to recover from Jen's loss was continuing to work on cases. Unfortunately, David did not agree and very soon, after Jen's death, kept losing interest in any type of attorney work. Nevertheless, he continued to work on his caseload and consult with the other less-experienced firm attorneys. Marc continued their close friendship and always left the door open for David's possible return to the active practice of jury trial work.

Grady was glad to see Marc and raised his paw as if to shake. Since Marc was ignoring the gesture, Grady's paw kept making contact with Marc's knee. He finally scratched the dog's head behind the ears, and Grady seem satisfied but continued to crave any attention.

Marc had a surgical mask dangling from his pocket. He said, "Things aren't the way they used to be. You have to appear in court with a mask. How's the fucking jury going to read your emotions if all they can see is your eyes? The judges don't seem to think it's a problem, but I surely do. I can't imagine you trying a jury trial with a mask."

David shook his head. "I never had to do that, and I cannot predict how a jury would react." David looked directly and candidly at Marc and said, "I'm not going to be able to find out either. It's been a while now since I tried my last jury trial for our practice, and I cannot see any way that I'm going to go back. My last wrongful death trial may be my very last. I'm sorry, Marc. I know you want things to be the way that they were, but that's not going to happen.

"I think the COVID-19 epidemic has given me time and an opportunity to reflect on both Jen's death and where I want to be after her death. I've had time to work on her dream house and landscape. It was more therapeutic than I thought it would be. It seems like it is my house now too. This pandemic has killed millions, and we may just be at the beginning. As selfish as it sounds, it has also given me space and time to reflect. Before I met Maeva, I had thought of moving, but I don't know where I'd go at this point. I want you to know that I've been grateful for your friendship, both personally and professionally."

Marc held up his hands. "This is purely a social call. I wanted to see how you're doing." He looked over the landscape and said, "I had forgotten how green and gorgeous the grounds around your house could look in full bloom. You put your COVID isolation to good work."

David smiled. "Would you like a beer or something from the refrigerator? You know where it is."

Marc shook his head as if to decline the offer.

Grady barked again, looked through the sliding glass door into the kitchen, and immediately started whining again.

Maeva slid the glass door open and stepped out onto the patio. She said, "Mr. Goodman," and smiled.

She put a hand on each of his shoulders, and he replied, with feigned formality, "Ms. Sopo, I was hoping to see you." Goodman gave her a peck on the cheek and placed his hands on her outstretched arms, near her biceps.

She was an impressive woman. He was 5'9" tall, and she looked him directly in the eyes despite the fact she had discarded her shoes somewhere. Her figure had always reminded him of an Olympic swimmer with broad, smooth shoulders; a slim waist; and powerful legs. She was dressed conservatively in a white blouse and gray skirt. Maeva either wore no makeup, or it was quite minimal. There may have been some lip gloss on her broad dark lips. Her hair was shoulder-length, jet black, and somewhat wavy. A summer tan made her brown skin seem deeper and healthier. She disengaged from Goodman's friendly touch and approached David. He rose, kissed her warmly, and they embraced briefly.

"I need a run, and Grady looks like he could use one too." Grady recognized the word *run* and started whining and twisting in a circle. "If you gentlemen will excuse me, we will both return happier and calmer." She glanced down at David's can of ale and said, "Did I interrupt legal talk or just drinking?"

"A little bit of both, honey." David smiled.

When the sliding glass door had closed, Marc said, "We have just a month to give the Colorado Trial Lawyers a draft of your seminar outline on the timing and dynamics of a successful personal-injury settlement. Do you see any problem with that deadline?"

"Don't worry, I have plenty of time and an open calendar. It may be my last attempt at anything law-related. I will do my best to drum up some referrals for Goodman and Richards, PC, to leave as my legacy. Besides, I can basically give the same speech that I gave to the defense lawyers last year. That outline is still on my computer upstairs."

CHAPTER 2

Maeva clicked on Grady's halter and walked him down David's driveway. When she reached the street, she immediately started running. Grady was trained to stay to her left, by her side. He loved to run and matched her stride. They ran on the street for approximately a quarter mile until they found the entrance to a conservation easement. It was a dirt path that traveled to the north among cottonwood trees that lined the valley stream. It was a perfect surface for running. She was used to running in the early morning when she often encountered mule deer, owls, and an occasional raccoon. In the late afternoon, she and Grady had the trail to themselves.

It had been a hectic day, and she was hoping that the run would calm her nerves. She heard the lilting call of a meadowlark and smiled. Her boss, John "King" Kingsley, had been out for two days attending to his sick wife. Mrs. Kingsley was suffering from COPD due to years of smoking and was feeling the effects in her seventies.

During King's absence, Maeva had to field all the incoming calls from clients and reassure them that their case was progressing even in King's absence. She did not mind interfacing with the clients, but she also had to deal with King's number one associate, Irving Roth. He was an impeccably well-dressed and well-groomed slender man in his late twenties. In King's absence, he wanted to assume the role of the lawyer in charge of King's cases but didn't really want to put in any hard work.

To the staff of Kingsley and Associates, he was referred to as Irving the Douche due to his condescending attitude to all but King. He was content to be listed as the attorney of record on the firm's pleadings, under King's name, so that he could attend court proceedings as counsel of record. However, as King had confided in Maeva and others, he wanted to play the game of being a trial attorney but did not want to get his uniform dirty with actual conflict.

When King was not in the office, Roth would try to listen in on Maeva's conversations with clients or court personnel so that he could monitor the progress of the case without actually doing any work. He would then review her computer notes. Roth would follow up with lengthy memos to Maeva, purporting to give her direction and supervision.

In reality, King entrusted Maeva with every aspect of his caseload and counted on her to make all the necessary decisions in his absence. Maeva was content to let Irving the Douche think he was managing the caseload even though he fulfilled no substantive role. He still irritated her every day.

As Maeva was running down the dirt trail with Grady beside her, she wondered about how the Native Americans survived in this environment. She was French Polynesian from the island of Huahine. There, fruits like citrons, mangos, and bananas were available for picking and eating at any time. Here, amid the cottonwood trees and prairie grass, nothing edible was readily apparent. There must have been some hidden roots and berries. She couldn't imagine the Native Americans surviving solely on deer, squirrels, and wild turkey. Maybe they ate frogs and crawdads from the streams. Unless the flora and fauna had changed significantly from when the native tribes roamed these plains, it must have been a very difficult existence.

Maeva's presence in Colorado was an improbable one. She was the only daughter of Tahitian Polynesian parents who were born and raised in Huahine. Her parents were in their late thirties when Maeva arrived as somewhat of a surprise. Her father was a fisherman and was often gone from the home for extended periods of time. They lived fairly traditionally in the jungle forest in a hut constructed out of wood and broad leaves that needed constant repair.

Maeva's mother took care of the home, prepared the meals, and tended their chickens and an occasional pig. Her mother was significantly overweight and was suffering the effects of diabetes even when Maeva was quite young.

As her mother's weight and deconditioning increased, Maeva's responsibilities and caregiving increased. It was young Maeva's job to gather the eggs in the morning, harvest fresh fruit and coconuts, and make sure the animals were fed and did not stray too far from their homesite. She also had to walk to the Chinese store in their vicinity to fetch the baguettes and cookies for her mother.

Over time, her father rarely appeared at home. Maeva was told that he was on extended fishing trips, but she could sense that their bond was dissolving. When her father failed to show up for several months, Maeva was told that her father had drowned in a fishing accident. Mother and child were eventually befriended by LDS missionaries on their island. Maeva was offered elementary school courses in French and Tahitian in a nearby village, and her mother was presented with regular boxes of food and clothing.

When Maeva returned from classes in the afternoon, she would often find that her mother had not moved from her mattress. One day when she came home, she found her mother lifeless and unresponsive. Maeva tried to give her water and cookies, but her mother was gone. Maeva lay next to her body until the missionaries came to check on her two days later.

There was a brief funeral. Word spread fast, and she had many relatives show up for the service whom she had never seen before. Family members offered to adopt the pretty but independent young girl. She was obviously bright and was a hard worker.

Instead of going to live with a family member, Maeva decided to go with the LDS missionaries to a boarding school on the island of Mo'orea. Although it was lonely at first, she soon learned to immerse herself in reading. She read French books and magazines but also began to learn English. After all, English was the first language of her missionary mentors. She read everything she could get in English, including the Book of Mormon. She impressed her instructors with her intelligence and curiosity. Her retention and ability to express herself in writing made her stand out from other students.

Maeva initially visited her relatives on Huahine every month or two and enjoyed being with her cousins. However, she eventually moved on to her secondary education and visited Huahine less and less. English became her primary language, and she used French only when necessary in the community. The LDS missionaries had a powerful presence in Tahiti and nurtured their historic bond with the Polynesians. Maeva was a offered a scholarship to attend the University of Utah, which the missionary instructors encouraged her to accept.

Without knowing anything about the United States other than what the LDS missionaries had taught her or that which she had read, she agreed to move to the United States to continue her education. The church was generous and provided her with clothing and an allowance while she continued her studies. She felt a tremendous amount of guilt when she decided to transfer to the University of Colorado and leave the Utah LDS community.

She sensed that she had been living in a bubble. Her grades were so good that, in addition to her minority status as a Pacific Islander, she was readily accepted to the University of Colorado School of Business and was offered additional scholarships. It was in Colorado that she learned of paralegal training. Her unusual minority status and aptitude once again opened doors to the paralegal world. Kingsley and Associates, PC, offered her an apprenticeship, and she worked her way up to be the paralegal to John Kingsley, the senior partner and sole shareholder, who had been impressed with both her work ethic and legal writing and research skills. In time, Kingsley preferred to work with her over seasoned associate attorneys.

Maeva realized she had chosen a more complicated and stressful lifestyle than she had in French Polynesia by coming to Colorado and getting involved in the legal world. On the plus side of her life ledger, her choices had allowed her the financial freedom to own her own townhome in Greenwood Village, an upscale suburb of Denver. She drove a new Mazda SUV.

Most importantly, Maeva felt professionally successful and independent. Now she even had a loving and satisfying relationship with David Richards. That was something that she had not previously allowed herself. The only negative in her career was the perception that she had overachieved her training and experience and owed everything to her relationship with Kingsley.

She smiled as she continued to run down the country path and look down at Grady. Her stress continued to melt away through exercise. Even this dog had become precious to her. In some ways, the COVID-19 pandemic had allowed her and David the necessary time and isolation to have developed their relationship. Although Kingsley and Associates had recently demanded that its employees mask up, practice social distancing, and continue to work in the office, she had ample time to spend with David and Grady in the country.

She still maintained her townhome but usually spent several nights a week at David's house. They had set up a separate home office for her with all the equipment necessary to telecommute. He had a full gym in the unfinished part of his basement which allowed her to get her early-morning workouts. She generally alternated between resistance training on one day and cardiovascular training on the next day.

When she was not at David's house, a full gym was available to her in the Kingsley and Associates' office building. Physical fitness was an important part of her lifestyle. Her island people had a tendency to put on weight, and she was determined to use diet and exercise to maintain the lean-and-healthy muscular physique that she had developed since moving away from Huahine and Mo'orea.

At two miles out, Maeva turned around and headed back for David's house.

CHAPTER 3

When she got back to David's house, Maeva quickly headed for the shower and some fresh clothes. Taking a shower at David's house was a luxurious experience—at least, if you were in the shower off of the master bedroom. He had an extra-large shower enclosure, eight by five feet, with two shower heads. The tile of the shower had different hues of green travertine and was very soothing. She lingered until the adjoining bathroom area became warm and steamy.

She wrapped herself in a large bath towel which had been hanging next to the glass shower door. When she emerged from the shower, she saw David standing in the bathroom area, shirtless and smiling. He took several slow steps and embraced her. They shared a long, hungry kiss. Maeva let the towel drop. Eventually, David cupped her breasts and touched her erect brown nipples to his pink ones. His 6'4" frame required him to lean forward to make the contact. She rubbed against him and laced her fingers behind his neck.

Continuing to kiss, they moved eagerly through the bathroom area to the master bedroom. The king-sized bed had been turned down. David lowered her slowly onto the cool sheets. He went to his knees and started to softly stroke her wavy black pubic thatch. Maeva sighed playfully. David parted her pubic hair with his hands and found her clit with his exploring tongue. Maeva moaned and started to pull David up from his kneeling position by the back of his armpits. David resisted and continued to expertly use his tongue.

After a few moments, her moaning became deeper, and David could feel the subtle muscle spasm as she reached her initial orgasm. He tried to continue, but she rolled onto the bed on her left side. She lifted her right thigh and said, "Come inside me." David cupped her right thigh on his bicep and positioned himself behind her so she could take his full length.

After he had come, they both lay on their backs on the cool sheets and glanced at the ceiling in the afterglow. Several silent minutes passed. Then they were aware of Grady softly whining from the threshold of the bedroom door. Maeva laughed. "Apparently someone is lonely or hungry." David propped himself up on his elbow. In response, Grady slowly approached their bed and placed his chin on the sheets.

After Grady supped, they made their own meal. It was a joint effort. David sliced skinless-and-boneless chicken breasts, shallots, and mangoes. Maeva had her own herb mixture for the chicken. When she had dredged the meat with the herb mixture, she lowered the strips into heated coconut oil. David then added the shallots and mangoes. Maeva held up an unpeeled mango, shook her head, and said, "I cannot believe that we have to pay for a piece of fruit like this." Maeva shook her head derisively. "Back home, these are the ones that we would throw out." Soon the cooking mixture filled the kitchen with a delicious aroma.

"I can always get us some fresh tomatoes from the low garden," David replied.

"Not quite the same thing, but thank you, dear."

There would be plenty of dinner for both of them. Maeva generally cooked enough so that she could take leftovers for lunch on the following day. Her diet consisted mostly of protein, fruits, or vegetables with very few carbohydrates. Maeva rarely ate bread or pasta. David had never seen her eat fast food or prepare any meal from a box. David was not as strict in his diet but was happy to share her recipes. She was a great cook, and he could appreciate the benefit of her low-carbohydrate intake. He had even unintentionally lost a bit of weight over the last year while sharing many weekly meals with her.

By the time they'd finished their meal and let Grady out into the backyard for his evening stroll, both were ready for bed. They fell asleep in each other's arms while a cool breeze flowed through the master bedroom from open windows. There was very little light other than moonlight in that part of Elbert County. The night sounds were usually crickets, toads, or the howl of a coyote. Often you could hear the hooting of a great-horned owl that would sit on David's roof in the early mornings. It was an ideal sleeping environment.

In the morning, David awoke to the sound of the shower. Maeva had already eaten her breakfast, worked out in David's basement gym, and was getting ready to travel the twenty-five miles to the Greenwood Village office of Kingsley and Associates.

Some of the benefits of semiretirement were waking up whenever he wanted, working out whenever he wanted, and setting his own daily schedule. He had once followed Maeva's early morning routine but no longer felt compelled to do so. That day, he feigned sleep and waited to hear the front door close.

Feeling slightly lazy and guilty, he got up and found Grady's leash for their run. He did not have to say the word *run* twice.

CHAPTER 4

John Kingsley did not feel like a king that morning. He had not been able to attend to his practice for the last few days because his wife was having respiratory difficulties. She always had some degree of difficulty breathing due to her smoking history. They had both smoked when they were married in their twenties, but King quit his cigarette habit before age thirty. He found that it interfered with his ability to play tennis and golf the way he wanted to play, which was always competitively.

His wife, Kathy, continued to smoke into her late sixties when she developed emphysema. Based upon her age and her respiratory challenges, she was a member of the vulnerable population to the COVID-19 virus. She would be one of the populations that would receive the initial accelerated vaccines promised by the end of the year by the politicians. King had recently started to wear a mask whenever he was indoors and reluctantly required everyone in his office to wear a mask as well.

As usual, Maeva had been in the office before King had arrived. Irving Roth never arrived until after 9:00 a.m. Maeva was working on exhibits for an upcoming product liability trial in U.S. district court. She was always organized and prepared in advance for any court proceeding or deposition. All King had to do was open a computer file and find the documents and evidence summaries necessary for each step of the case. King rarely had to instruct Maeva on the next step of trial preparation.

In over forty years of practice, he had never known a legal assistant or even an associate attorney who was more valuable to his trial practice. He felt that she could have easily gone into court and tried a case on her own. He had sincerely suggested that she consider law school and had offered to provide her with the time and tuition. However, Maeva gratefully declined and indicated she was doing what she wanted to do as his assistant. She appreciated the fact that it would have taken her at least ten years to rise to the level of compensation and authority that she enjoyed as King's personal legal assistant.

Irving Roth had no idea that Maeva Sopo earned more money and benefits than he did. After all, he was a third-year associate attorney, and she was only a paralegal/legal assistant.

King had a remarkable energy level for a trial attorney in his seventies. While most of his peers had retired or slowed down to part-time senior status as a litigator, King continued a full docket of cases and tried several complex jury trials per year. Most considered him to have a photographic memory. He was always proud of the fact that he could memorize the names, occupations, and circumstances of each individual jury candidate as they were being questioned by the judge and/or attorneys in the voir dire process of jury selection. Often King's opposing counsel had to immediately apologize and explain that they were unable to accomplish this feat and had to rely on their written notes.

King picked up his telephone and punched in Maeva's extension number. "Can you come in here a moment, when you have the time, so that we can talk about the logistics of the Baker trial next week?"

King was just hanging up his telephone when Maeva entered the room. She sat down in a chair which was more than eight feet from King's desk. King said, "I'm sorry about you having to wear a mask in the office and keeping the social distancing these days."

"No worry. Most everyone is doing it these days. It is just our new normal." Maeva smiled with her eyes even though her mouth was covered.

"You healthy young people probably don't have to worry about getting sick. My wife, Kathy, is deathly afraid of even going to the supermarket these days. Everything seems to be delivered to our front porch. Then we have to wash all the packages down with bleach. She is completely isolated from friends and family. I have to do more on the home front, and I don't feel as up-to-date in the office." King bowed his head and ran his fingers through his thick kinky short hair. When he was younger, his hair had been dark red but was now mostly white with a slight pinkish hue.

Maeva said, "It is only temporary. Soon everyone will be vaccinated, and life will get back to normal. Wearing a mask and having to social distance isn't really that bad."

"It is hard for an old fart like me. I can't stand wearing a mask in court. It puts a barrier between me and the jury. I've always relied upon my conversational rapport with the jury and witnesses. The mask gets in the way."

"I have yet to notice any difference in your performance." Maeva approached his desk and handed him a folder with a summary of each witness' expected testimony in the Baker trial. The summaries were obtained from deposition transcripts and cross-referenced by line and page. King opened the folder and nodded. He appreciated the fact that she still reduced data to paper for him. It was his preferred method of preparation.

The Baker case was a product liability case. Their client was accused of manufacturing a pharmaceutical that caused serious neurological dysfunction in some patients. Their defense rested upon expert medical and scientific testimony to the effect that less than 1 percent of the population suffered adverse effects and that the premanufactured testing had been rigorous. Yvonne Baker, the plaintiff, was unfortunately the victim of irreversible brain damage that left her in a vegetative state. The case was potentially worth tens of millions of dollars.

King rose from his chair, walked around his desk, and handed the file back to Maeva for placement in their trial notebook. He took the moment to put his arm around her shoulder and give her a paternal hug. It was a rare thing for him to have physical contact with her, but she accepted the gesture. She placed her hand on his hand and said, "We will be ready to go to war as usual, masks and all." King gave her another hugging gesture and nodded his appreciation.

Irving Roth tentatively knocked on King's open office door. He smirked at their brief embrace and said, "I'm sorry that I missed the meeting. I also thought that we were practicing social distancing," he said, as if accidentally interrupting a romantic moment. "Do you need any witness preparation help for the Baker trial?"

King moved away from Maeva awkwardly and shook his head. "Maeva and I have that handled. Please make sure that all our exhibits are properly marked on the computer and ready for presentation to the court and jury."

"I will have them ready for you to review this afternoon."

Maeva nodded to Roth and walked past him in King's open door. King said, "Just e-mail them to Maeva so that she can make sure you have everything we need."

"Of course. Whatever she wants or needs." Roth's sarcastic tone was barely perceptible as he spoke through his paper surgical mask.

CHAPTER 5

Almost three years previously, David Richards was sitting across the street from the Comanche County District Court building, in the Comanche Café. The COVID-19 virus was not yet known or imagined. No masks were routinely worn in the United States, and no one had ever heard of social distancing. He was sitting with the court reporter and acting district court clerk, Rosa Diaz.

Rosa was smoking a long thin brown cigarette. Smoking was not allowed in restaurants, but she was Rosa Diaz, wife of the Comanche County sheriff and court reporter for the Comanche County Board of Commissioners, in addition to her district court clerk and reporter duties. She wore bright-red lipstick and sunglasses that were so dark you could not see her eyes. She wore tightfitting clothing to accentuate her full figure. In her mid-thirties, she was already a powerful and influential force in the rural county and wanted everyone to know that fact.

David always made it a point to either buy breakfast, lunch, or a drink for Rosa when he visited her county depending upon the time of day for his court appearance. She was always the best source for either court gossip or county news. Rosa had gotten to know David from the two trials he tried in Comanche County and liked him despite the fact that he was a Denver attorney. Most of the attorneys from Denver were arrogant and condescending to the Comanche County court personnel except for the judge. Everyone was always polite to the judge and laughed at his jokes.

"John David is cranky today," Rosa said. "He feels disrespected because you have disregarded his pretrial order that was entered when you filed the complaint. You served the complaint two months ago, yet there has been no official response from the defense attorney and you have not filed a motion for default." Rosa puffed on her cigarette and blew long plumes of smoke out through her aquiline nose. "If I were you, I would kiss some ass and get back into his good graces. He always has seemed to like you even though you're a Denver attorney."

"Thanks for the heads up, Rosa. Always appreciate your insights and comments."

Judge John David Keena was always fairly cranky. He was a recovering alcoholic and was prone to unpredictable rants and raves, directed mostly at the attorneys who were appearing in front of him. He had once been a candidate for US district judge and was bitter about the fact that his nomination was pulled back at the last moment by the nominating Colorado US senator. It was supposedly something about his politics on abortion issues.

David always thought Judge Keena still had a great position as a state district judge. Comanche County was large geographically but sparsely populated. He was the only district judge, a position with great local authority and general jurisdiction. His caseload was quite light compared to the metropolitan areas of the state, and he got to see a variety of criminal and civil matters.

Rosa and David finished their coffee. Rosa stubbed out her cigarette in the remainder of a chocolate-glazed doughnut on her plate. They walked across the two-laned street to the Comanche County Courthouse.

This courthouse was one of David's all-time favorites. It looked like a courthouse. It had granite steps and a granite façade. They entered through large bronze doors in the arched entryway. The interior of the courthouse was oak paneling halfway up the wall and painted plaster on the top half of the walls and ceiling. The individual courtrooms were also oak-paneled with high painted ceilings and brass light fixtures. The courtrooms had old-style railings and a large oak bench for the judge with the seal of the State of Colorado behind the bench between the flag of the United States of America and the State of Colorado. Counsel had plain wooden tables and oak barrel chairs which were not comfortable, but they were rustic. The courtroom had rows of solid oak pews for public seating.

Rosa entered the courtroom with her stenography machine. Many of the counties had gone to audio-recorded proceedings, but many rural Colorado courtrooms still had human court reporters. David had already taken a seat at the plaintiff's counsel's table. Rosa said, "The defense firm, the Kingsley firm, entered an electronic appearance this morning. I have yet to see King or anyone from his office."

David nodded his appreciation for the news. He knew King was going to be on the case. King and he had been negotiating a potential settlement for weeks. They had agreed, in concept, to the type of consideration that needed to be paid by the liability insurance company. However, King said he had difficulty getting the authority he needed from the claims manager of the insurer. David and King both knew the case was going to settle and that it would settle in the neighborhood they had discussed. It just had not happened yet. David knew that King was currently in a lengthy jury trial in US district court, but David had sent King's secretary a copy of Judge Keena's order for a scheduling conference that morning.

A young new associate of King's named Irving Roth entered the courtroom. He was followed by a tall dark woman whom David did not know. Counselor Roth was dressed in a very expensive and well-tailored wool suit. David and Roth knew each other from previous cases. Roth usually just carried King's briefcase or other materials necessary for a court appearance or deposition. Today he appeared to be the main lead attorney. He shook David's hand and sat down at the defense table.

David approached the tall dark woman and introduced himself as plaintiff's counsel. She shook his hand with a firm grip and stated, "I am a legal assistant at Kingsley and Associates. My name is Maeva Sopo." She was businesslike and barely made eye contact. The woman had a slight French accent. She wore a navy-blue blazer and skirt with a white blouse and black pumps. She had an aura of self-assurance but also seemed apprehensive about the court appearance.

Rosa Diaz said in a loud voice that resonated in the cavernous courtroom: "All rise, the Comanche County District Court is now in session. Judge John David Keena presiding."

A black-robed Judge Keena appeared and ascended the bench. He had thin, wispy salt-and-pepper hair and a stringy salt-and-pepper mustache. He glared at the individuals in the courtroom and said, "Where is Mr. Kingsley?"

The young attorney rose in response. "I am Irving Roth of the Kingsley and Associates law firm appearing on behalf of the defendant today. Mr. Kingsley is in the middle of a United States district court trial. We just received notice of this hearing."

"Apparently, that is a more important proceeding than this one today. Both counsel are either aware or should be aware of my pretrial order. An answer was to be filed within twenty days of service of the complaint upon the defendant. If not, either a motion from the defendant for an extension of time to respond was due within twenty days, or a motion for default was to be filed by the plaintiff. Neither occurred. I am prepared to hear a motion for default against the defendant, or a motion to dismiss plaintiff's complaint for failure to comply with the pretrial order. In fact, there has been a failure of both sides to comply with the court's pretrial order."

Maeva Sopo rose and, with a subdued voice, inquired, "Would the court mind if I digitally recorded these proceedings so that an accurate and appropriate order can be prepared?"

"Who the hell are you? That is off the record, Ms. Diaz." Judge Keena seemed very irritated with being interrupted. "Are you an attorney? Only attorneys address the court. No, you cannot record this hearing. Rosa Diaz is the district court reporter and the only individual authorized to record anything in this court. She knows what she is doing."

Rosa rolled her eyes for the benefit of the attorneys and Maeva. Maeva dutifully sat down and put her hands on the yellow legal pad in front of her.

David Richards stood and said, "If it pleases the court, I am aware of the contents of your pretrial order, and if there is anyone at fault, I will be the one to take that blame. Mr. Kingsley and I have been negotiating an out-of-court settlement and are very close to resolving all issues. Mr. Kingsley's firm entered an appearance this morning, as I have been informed, and a motion for default on the part of the plaintiff would be inappropriate in my view. I may have inadvertently led Mr. Kingsley's firm to believe that there was no need to file an answer or other responsive pleading while we were negotiating."

Judge Keena pursed his lips, stroked his mustache, and considered David's position. "Were you not aware, from the pretrial order, that informal agreements between counsel would not extend any time periods required by the Colorado Rules of Civil Procedure?"

"Yes, Your Honor, but we were very close to filing a stipulation regarding settlement prior to the expiration of your time limits. I knew Mr. Kingsley was in trial and could not get back to me to finalize our stipulation. All responsibility for any violation of your pretrial order is on the part of the plaintiff's counsel, me, and should not prejudice the defendant. If the court should dismiss the plaintiff's complaint, we are still within the statute of limitations, and we could refile. However, I want to assure the court that settlement is imminent and probable. I want to personally apologize for any inconvenience to both court and counsel."

Keena looked at Irving Roth and said, "What is the defendant's position?"

Roth rose from the defense counsel's table. "We concur with plaintiff's counsel." He sat down meekly as soon as those words were spoken.

Keena ruled, "The defense has three days to file a responsive pleading. I would suggest that it be an answer and not any pleading calculated to delay these proceedings any further. If no answer is filed within that time, plaintiff's counsel shall file a motion for default, and we will proceed on the issue of damages only, not liability.

"The Court is aware that this is a wrongful death case arising out of the plaintiff motorist striking the defendant rancher's bull on a county highway. The Court is further aware that there have been prior instances of the defendant's livestock being on the county roads and other motor vehicle accidents as a direct result. The Court sincerely doubts whether there's going to be any reasonable liability defense mounted in this case. Of course, I am not prejudging the evidence, but I am giving fair warning to counsel that we're not going to waste the Court's time on baseless legal arguments."

Keena turned his irritated gaze to Maeva and said, "I trust that you got the gist of my order, Missy. If not, Rosa Diaz will have a true-and-accurate transcription, which she can probably get to you within twenty-four hours."

Keena abruptly left the bench and retired to his chambers. David was packing up his documents when Maeva approached him with her hand outstretched. Another firm dry handshake. She said, "I want you to know that King will appreciate your help and professional courtesy when I tell him what happened."

David smiled. "He would've done the same for me, I have no doubt. We go back awhile. Judge Keena is a little difficult, but he rarely rules knowing that he is on shaky ground."

Roth was hurrying to exit and was almost at the courtroom door when Maeva turned to leave. She did not hurry, and David noticed that she moved with athletic fluidity and confidence.

Rosa Diaz picked up her stenography equipment, put her hand on David's forearm, and said, "I wonder how long King has had the island girl as an assistant? The judge was a little tough on her."

"She didn't seem to take it personally."

CHAPTER 6

I t was still pre-pandemic when David saw Maeva again. He was monitoring a case, along with Marc Goodman, in Pueblo County District Court. One of the TV law firms in Southern Colorado was called Joe Grimsby and Associates. Joe Grimsby had commercials on TV, radio, and billboards with his smiling face throughout the area. His firm brought in a huge volume of cases from this area, but his law firm rarely went to trial on serious cases that had a high verdict potential. Those he referred out to seasoned and successful trial lawyers, such as Goodman and Richards, PC. That day, both David Richards and Marc Goodman were present in the courtroom to hear arguments on the defendant's motion for summary judgment.

Joe Grimsby was an exceptional businessman and knew how to evaluate a case for its damages award potential. He was not as good in assessing the potential legal liability of the defendants. The case he was litigating that day had great damage potential. The defendants, local ranchers, and landowners had an adult son who worked as a ranch foreman. The ranch had been the victim of modern-day cattle rustling.

One night, the adult son could see flashlight beams and vehicle headlights in one of his parents' distant pastures. He grabbed one of his parents' Winchester .30-30 rifles, jumped in a pickup truck, and went to investigate. As he neared the pasture, the flashlight and headlight beams were still evident. He could not tell whether they had actually loaded up some of his parents' cattle yet. He decided to stop his pickup truck and fire a warning shot at the trespassers. He did not fire at any of the beams but fairly close to the left.

Unfortunately, he heard a scream, and all the flashlight beams were quickly pointed to the area where the shot was directed. The sound of an engine starting could be heard in the pasture. The distant vehicle was moving without headlights. When the foreman arrived at the area, there was no vehicle present. However, several Hispanic males were standing over a man lying in the field. They had removed their straw cowboy hats and were upset and grieving. The man on the ground was either dead or dying from a gunshot wound to the chest.

Joe Grimsby had filed a civil wrongful death lawsuit. The only defendant was the adult son foreman. The civil complaint had alleged that he had intentionally and/or recklessly shot the decedent. The foreman had previously been criminally charged and convicted of reckless homicide and was serving time in a Colorado prison.

Grimsby had taken a civil default judgment against the foreman for millions in compensatory and punitive damages. However, Grimsby had not thought out the fact that intentional acts were excluded from any potential liability insurance coverage. The foreman's son had no ownership interest in the ranch and had no funds or insurance coverage to satisfy the judgment. He had used his meager savings to mount an unsuccessful defense to the criminal charges. Now, Joe Grimsby was trying to bring the parents into the lawsuit as landowners, including their liability insurance carrier, on the theory that they had negligently allowed or ignored dangerous activities on their ranch.

Joe Grimsby did not relish appearing in court against a seasoned defense attorney. In this case, the defense counsel was Kingsley and Associates, one of the state's best defense firms. When King had entered his appearance, Grimsby immediately contacted Goodman and Richards, PC, for litigation purposes.

David Richards and Marc Goodman were cautious. Today's ruling on the defendant's motion for summary judgment would determine whether or not they wanted to take on this potentially valuable case.

Joe Grimsby approached Marc Goodman and said, "You guys could enter your appearance today and argue the summary judgment motion." He was a slight man and had one of the most unbelievably horrible toupees that Marc Goodman had ever seen. It sat perched upon his head and was a completely darker shade of brown than the natural hair on the side of his head which had turned lighter and grayer. On Grimsby's billboard advertisements, the hair and toupee appeared to be the same shade and texture.

"David and I have decided to wait and see how this proceeding develops before making a final decision. We are not going to enter our appearance at this time, and we will just be observing today. We already discussed that with your secretary."

Grimsby looked in David's direction. David nodded his head as if to concur with his partner. Grimsby shook his head with disappointment and planted himself at the plaintiff's counsel's table.

Irving Roth, accompanied by Maeva Sopo, entered the Pueblo District Courtroom and sat at the defendant's counsel's table. This was a very modern courthouse. It was all stainless steel and glass. The judge's bench and counsel's tables were made of black recycled glass and steel. Pueblo County was a relatively densely populated county for Southern Colorado and had a very busy docket.

The judge's clerk/bailiff was a young Hispanic male, probably a law student. He said his name was David Suazo and invited the parties to enter the judge's chamber. David Richards and Marc Goodman remained in the courtroom.

After a few minutes, Mr. Suazo returned to the courtroom and indicated that the judge would permit the two of them to observe argument in his chambers. Both Marc Goodman and his law partner were well-known to the judge, and he understood that they were monitoring the case to determine whether they wanted to substitute as plaintiff's counsel.

The judge was Chadwick Lemmon. He had been one of the youngest judges ever to be appointed to the bench in Colorado and was only now in his mid-forties despite having served over eight years as a Pueblo County district judge. He smiled as David Richards and Mark Goodman entered his chambers and said, "I understand that both of you gentlemen are considering whether to enter your appearance in this case. I'm sure that the outcome of today's hearing will make a big difference. Rather than having someone explain what happened or having to order the transcript of the proceedings, I thought it might be easier to just have you observe. Please refrain from making any comments or consulting with the attorneys."

"Thank you, judge," David said as he sat next to Marc on one of four steel chairs in the corner of the judge's spacious chambers.

"We are here today on the defendant's motion for summary judgment. As you know, that motion requires the court to determine whether there are any genuine material issues of fact to be litigated, or whether the defendants are entitled to judgment as a matter of law. I have read the briefs. I am giving you an opportunity to supplement your legal briefs with any argument you wish to submit. This will be informal. We are not on the record, and there is no court reporter present. I do not consider any arguments put forth in the chambers as anything other than an informal explanation of your respective clients' written position in the briefs. If, at any time, either party wishes to put anything on the record, I will activate the digital recorder, and you can make any record that you deem appropriate. Otherwise, this will be a supplemental discussion of the legal issues." Judge Lemmon nodded to both counsels.

"I will first hear from the moving party, the defendant. I note that Mr. Kingsley is not present today. Who will be handling the argument for Kingsley and Associates?"

Irving Roth stood up and informed the court that Mr. Kingsley had a medical emergency. He was attending to his ill wife who had recently been hospitalized. The judge nodded, told Roth to sit down, and advised all counsel that it was not necessary to stand when addressing the court in chambers. "Proceed, Mr. Roth."

Before Roth could make any statement, Maeva leaned forward with her digital recorder in her hand and asked whether it would be permissible to record the proceedings for any proposed orders. Judge

Lemmon shrugged his shoulders and said, "Of course. Counsel can feel free to record any portion of this informal conference. Nothing said in these chambers is evidence, and it can only help refresh our memories if necessary."

Surprisingly, Roth quickly said, "Everything is set forth in our brief, Your Honor."

Judge Lemmon turned toward Joe Grimsby and said, "Would plaintiff's counsel like to add anything to the briefs?"

Joe Grimsby started to stand and then sat down again. He cleared his throat and said, "Judge, the crux of the defendants' argument is that the two-year statute of limitations has run on the complaint against the parents: Mr. and Mrs. Rodriguez, the landowners. It's our position that the filing of the original complaint against the defendants' adult son tolled the statute of limitation and that the filing of the original complaint against the parents was well within the two-year statute of limitation. It would be unfair to dismiss the claims against the parents when they arise out of the same factual circumstances." Grimsby sat down.

The judge turned to Irving Roth and said, "Anything in response, Mr. Roth?"

"We will stand on our briefs as submitted, Your Honor."

Judge Lemmon sat back in his chair behind his stainless steel and glass desk. He put his feet up on the desk and looked toward Roth. "Did you write the briefs in this case, Mr. Roth? I know Mr. Kingsley, and I've never seen him fail to take an opportunity to further his legal argument."

"I always review the briefs that are submitted, whether I write them or not."

Judge Lemmon looked at Maeva and said, "Did you research and write the briefs that Mr. Roth says he reviewed?"

Maeva self-consciously leaned closer to the judge and said, "I'm not an attorney. Yes, I researched the issues and prepared a draft of the brief, but I'm only a paralegal or legal assistant."

Grimsby spoke. "I object to a paralegal addressing the legal issues."

Judge Lemmon smiled and said, "Really? You want me to turn on the audio recording and allow you to put your position on the record? If I understand your position, you don't think the court should hear from someone who actually researched the legal issues and drafted the briefs? Ms. Sopo has already disclosed that she served in the capacity of a legal assistant while researching and drafting the briefs that were submitted. I will gladly turn on the audio recording if that is your position."

Grimsby said, "No, Your Honor, that will not be necessary."

Judge Lemmon looked at Maeva and said, "Ms. Sopo?"

"Your Honor, the cases cited in the plaintiff's briefs referred to situations where a corporate defendant had been served with the complaint before the statute of limitations expired. In some cases, the corporate defendant is misidentified or is a subsidiary of the named defendant. In those cases, the courts have held that the corporate defendant was put on actual notice of the allegations of liability by the original complaint and should be required to respond even if the correct corporate entity was not fully identified until after the statute of limitations has expired. That makes perfect sense in that factual scenario.

"However, here we have Mr. and Mrs. Rodriguez, the landowners, our clients, who were never served within the two-year statute of limitations. They did know that their son had been served with the complaint and had been previously convicted on criminal charges. They also knew that a civil default judgment was taken based upon his alleged intentional conduct. They were never involved in the civil case. Now more than two years after the incident, plaintiff's counsel is attempting to add them to the prior lawsuit against their son based upon a completely different legal theory of liability. They certainly had no notice of their own alleged liability within the two-year period. The original complaint was based upon allegations of their son's intentional acts, and nothing about the civil complaint against their son would have put them on notice of their potential liability as landowners for allowing a dangerous condition on their property."

Joe Grimsby stood up, shrugged his shoulders, and protested, "Overly simplistic analysis."

David Richards looked at his law partner, leaned over, and whispered in his ear, "Aren't we glad that we didn't get officially involved in this case?"

Marc Goodman nodded and returned the whisper, "King would've wiped the floor with Grimsby, but his legal assistant did a nice job too. What is Roth? A potted plant?"

Judge Lemmon glanced dismissively at Grimsby, declaring, "This Court must also be analyzing the situation simplistically. Waiting until after the statute of limitations expired to join new defendants on a new theory of liability is just too late as a matter of law. The defendants' motion is well-taken, and I will grant the motion for summary judgment. Will you, Mr. Roth or Ms. Sopo, draft an order granting defendant's motion for summary judgment? I believe that you have a recording of the proceedings. If the Grimsby firm needs a copy, please provide them with the recording by email."

Both Irving Roth and Maeva Sopo nodded their heads and said, "Yes, Your Honor," simultaneously. Roth was red-faced. He picked up his briefcase and immediately headed for the chambers' exit. Joe Grimsby followed Roth out the door.

Judge Lemmon stood up and said, "Thank you, counsel. Ms. Sopo, I was sorry to put you on the spot, but you rose to the occasion. Tell Mr. Kingsley that I hope that his wife is feeling better and that he was well-represented at this proceeding today."

"If she doesn't tell King, I will," said Marc Goodman. "I doubt that Mr. Roth will give Mr. King the full picture."

Maeva walked through the security lines near the courthouse exit. Marc and David were walking behind her. When they got to the parking lot, they saw and heard a BMW sedan exit the parking lot with screeching tires.

Maeva turned to David and Mark and said with a sardonic tone, "That would be Roth. That would be my ride. I guess it might also be my job."

CHAPTER 7

"No worry," Marc Goodman said as they were walking through the Pueblo Justice Center parking lot. "David has a Chevy Tahoe that has front and back seats as big as the couch in your living room. We're going back to the Denver Tech Center. We have plenty room, and it is no hassle."

David could sense that Maeva was tense. He decided to lighten the tone of the situation. "I have detected a slight French accent. Where are you from? I mean, originally?"

"My home is the island of Huahine in French Polynesia. It's part of what you probably identify as Tahiti." She got to David's Tahoe and started to open the backdoor. Marc Goodman shook his head and opened the front door for her. She slid into the front seat. She continued, "Tahitian and French were my first languages, which probably accounts for my accent."

David, still hoping to lighten the tone of the conversation, said, "I am not familiar with the name Sopo. Is that a Polynesian name? I am pretty sure that Maeva is French."

"Maeva is a fairly common name in French Polynesia. Sopo is a shortened version of my real Polynesian name. She pronounced the name in a long and clipped Polynesian accent. I shortened it so that you *haoles* could pronounce it. Spelling it is even harder with the punctuation necessary." She typed her surname into her phone and showed it to both Marc and David as the engine started.

Goodman laughed in the backseat, typed something into his cell phone, and passed it on to Maeva in the front seat. "Try that one on for size. That's my Hebrew name. Make sure to read it right to left."

Maeva showed the Hebrew characters to David, and they all laughed.

David said, "I wish I could remember how to spell the town where my Welsh ancestors came from. It is, like, all consonants and no vowels."

The drama of the Pueblo courthouse had dissipated. The trio headed up Interstate 25 to Denver with only lighthearted conversation.

Irving Roth had used his cell phone text to report to his clients that Kingsley and Associates had successfully dismissed the plaintiff's claims on their summary judgment motion. He noted that he had appeared as lead counsel. He also left a voicemail on King's mobile phone. He emailed some dictation to the office so that it could be transcribed and forwarded to the clients as soon as possible. Defeating a wrongful death claim on summary judgment would be a major victory, and he wanted to make sure that the client and the liability insurance company heard about it from his correspondence.

The next day, Maeva said nothing to Irving Roth about leaving her in Pueblo. She also said nothing when she overheard Roth telling King about how the plaintiff's complaint had been dismissed following oral argument. She listened to her own voice recorder and typed up an order for the judge's signature. The order merely incorporated their motion for summary judgment brief and did not discuss any of the argument which took place in the judge's chambers.

"Damn good brief, Maeva," King said as he passed her desk. "That is what won the day."

King looked older and tired. His usual high energy level had been sapped. Maeva noticed that his hands were shaking as he was going through the paperwork that had been placed on his desk. Despite his apparent distress, King put on his coat, took his briefcase, and headed off to US district court in downtown Denver for a day of trial. He could always draw the line between home and the office.

When Maeva saw Roth in the coffee room later that day, he did not apologize or offer any explanation for having left her in the Pueblo courthouse parking lot. He said, "Good job. A legal assistant doesn't get to speak in court very often. You must feel good. The old man is happy with both of us, and I'm sure the client is thrilled. I'm sure you're still the golden-brown girl in King's eyes."

Maeva said nothing. She filled her coffee cup and walked past Roth, who was lingering in the doorway. He consistently proved himself to be the Douche.

CHAPTER 8

Maeva and David did not see each other again until they both attended a Colorado defense lawyer's seminar in Steamboat Springs, Colorado. David was going to be a featured speaker on the topic of pretrial, trial, and posttrial settlement strategies. He was well-known to most of the defense lawyers who represented insurance companies and self-insured corporations. David had a reputation of being an exceptionally capable trial lawyer but also reasonable in his approach to settlement. Although Goodman and Richards, PC, was a plaintiff's personal injury law firm, the defense lawyers appreciated David's amiable insights into settlement opportunities from a plaintiff's perspective.

Marc Goodman had arranged this seminar to see if he could help mitigate David's loss. Jen had been killed in the car accident almost a year before, and David had rarely left his home in Elbert County except to visit their office. He seemed to be content with the company of his dog, Grady, out in the country. Marc was afraid that David was becoming a hermit in his grief and encouraged him to take the seminar.

Sarah Spenser, a defense lawyer in her early thirties, had organized David's participation in the seminar. She was a petite, attractive, short blonde woman with a high energy level and was very solicitous toward David. David had arrived the day before his speech and was shown around the hotel and seminar site by Ms. Spenser. It was summer, and the aspen and foliage were lush and green. The hotel had a spectacular view of Mt. Werner and was near the empty ski slopes.

Spenser knew David from two cases where they were opposing counsel. She also knew that he was a recent widower and had not been trying many jury trials in the past year. When she showed him the dais from where he would speak, she touched his right arm bicep and lightly massaged his arm. When she showed him the microphone, her left breast brushed the same bicep. She smiled warmly as he acknowledged the contact.

"I will have to chair the seminar's opening-night dinner this evening. Perhaps we can get together tomorrow at some point." Sarah rubbed David's left bicep this time, turned, and started walking away. She looked over her left shoulder and smiled.

David arose early the next morning and went to the hotel's exercise facility. He had just restarted his early morning exercise routine since Jen's death and found that it helped get his metabolism going and mitigated his depression. It was barely past six o'clock in the morning when he used his hotel room card to open the hotel exercise room door. He recognized a female figure in a black sleeveless leotard working out on the circuit machines. It was Maeva Sopo. She looked up at him and smiled in recognition, but then continued to concentrate on her work out without comment. David noticed that she had a small native island art tattoo on the top of her left shoulder.

David started his warm-up routine with dumbbells. The entire exercise room was paneled in mirrors. He noticed Maeva observing him as he continued his warm-up.

Sarah Spenser was the next person to enter the exercise facility. Despite the early morning, Sarah was fully made up and dressed in a new white cotton exercise outfit and electric green athletic shoes. She approached David and tried to start up a conversation. David was polite, replied, but continued his warm-up routine. Sarah seemed unsure about the surroundings but eventually adjusted an exercise bike seat and started to pedal slowly while watching a morning network television show on one of the many strategically located flatscreen sets on the walls of the gymnasium.

David continued his routine, alternately using the resistance machines and free weights. Sarah Spenser spoke to him between his sets. David responded but was obviously focused on his workout. After working about twenty minutes on her exercise bicycle, Sarah decided to leave. She told him she would see him later.

Maeva had also continued her workout without any conversation. She was focused and had a sheen of sweat. David had never seen her in anything but business attire and was impressed with her muscular physique. She was obviously an experienced weightlifter. She had the shape of a swimmer's body with wide well-developed shoulders, a fairly narrow waist, and muscular thighs and calves. It is a myth that women who are weightlifters will develop into bulky muscular types that resemble a male physique. That does not happen without the use of male hormones. Even the female bodybuilding competitions generally separate the hormone-enhanced females from those women with natural female muscular physiques. Maeva's was clearly the latter. Although muscular and well-defined, she was neither bulky nor masculine in her form.

Maeva was in such good shape and intense in her workout that she made David feel a little self-conscious. Although David had a home gym in his basement, he had not been as regular a user as he wanted to be. He had once been a college football player years ago and had the benefit of some of the finest trainers at the University of Colorado when he had played tight end for the Buffaloes for two years. A ruptured Achilles tendon had ended his football aspirations in his sophomore year. Although no longer a player, he tried to continue a workout routine to maintain his conditioning. Following Jen's accident, he had stopped working out for a while. Although he had started again a few weeks ago, he felt pudgy and flaccid.

Maeva apparently finished her routine. She picked up a fresh towel from a stack on the wall, wiped her face, and approached David who was doing bicep curls with dumbbells. She said, "I think Ms. Spenser was looking for a different type of workout this morning. She seemed to be a little disappointed."

David glanced at her without comment. He placed the dumbbells back on the wall rack. He finally said, "What brings you to Steamboat Springs? Do you need the continuing legal education credits?"

"I do not need credits, but King sent me up here. This is usually the seminar he attends because he can get all his yearly credits at once, over two and a half days. He is getting ready for trial, so this summer, I am on my own, taking notes and looking for some content that King will find useful."

"You can probably skip my portion. King has forgotten more about settlement strategy than I've ever learned."

Maeva wiped her forehead with a towel and said, "I am supposed to take notes and get a DVD of your presentation."

David put down his dumbbells. "I will be happy to review your notes."

Maeva put the towel underneath her damp black hair, behind her neck, and turned to leave the exercise room. "King would prefer my summary and impressions."

CHAPTER 9

David was midway through his presentation when he realized that this was something that Marc Goodman should be doing. Marc had done this seminar before, and he knew where to insert the lines that would result in laughter. However, David felt empty and mechanical. When he finished his lecture, many of the defense lawyers that he had litigated against or had cases with came up to the lectern and shook his hand and wanted to chat. Sarah Spenser mounted the dais and stood behind him while he spoke to those who wanted a direct conversation.

After he had spoken with all who lingered for personal access, David descended the dais and surveyed the room. Sarah followed him closely and placed a hand on his back. She said, "We are having drinks in the common area. I will see you there." She left the auditorium with the lingering promise of future contact. David noticed Maeva sitting at one of the tables, writing in her notebook.

David approached Maeva's table and stood a respectful distance from her. He said, "There is a trail south of the ski area that goes over a hill where there's a large meadow. We might be able to see elk and

perhaps even moose if we get there before sundown. Are you interested in a walk?"

"What about the cocktail hour? Sarah will be expecting you.
And don't gentlemen prefer blondes?"

"No. And what makes you think that I'm a gentleman? I just
thought that an island girl might appreciate the opportunity to view
some mountain fauna."

"This island girl has lived in both Utah and Colorado for a
while. I always like to see elk, but I've never seen a moose in the wild.
Let's give it a try. Let me get out of my paralegal outfit and into my
leisure gear. I'll meet you in the front of the hotel in twenty minutes."

*****

They were both in shorts and T-shirts when they met at the
front of the hotel. The sun was still bright but would disappear
quickly on the mountainous horizon to the west. Within a month,
autumn would be approaching, and they would have needed to wear
jackets and long pants as soon as the sun set. For now, the August sun
would keep the mountain air warm after dark. They walked along a
well-defined trail to the south of a dormant ski lift and ascended the
hill to the meadow that David had described. It was still light but
dimming, as the sun was sinking into the mountainous horizon.

Maeva was ahead on the trail as they neared the crest that would
give them a view of the meadow below. David was several feet behind
her when he saw the head of a black bear rise above the brush in
silhouette. The bear was standing fully erect, six feet tall, and was
clearly surprised by the hikers. Then two smaller black bear cub
heads appeared on either side of the sow.

David lurched ahead, grabbed Maeva's forearm, and said, "Run.
Run downhill now. Do not look back and keep going downhill until
we reach the flat area. Bears don't like to run downhill, and sows do
not like to leave their babes unattended."

They both ran faster than they thought they could down a dirt
and rock trail. They both stopped when the trail flattened, and when

there was no mother bear behind them, they both started laughing hysterically.

"You suck as a nature guide." Maeva pushed his shoulder. David took her arm, looked up the trail again, and then pulled her toward him. He kissed her deeply. She responded fully with eager and moist broad lips. He took her hand, and they walked slowly toward the hotel without speaking. When they got to the lobby of the hotel, Maeva said, "I'm sure that your suite is bigger and fancier, but no one's going to come knocking on my door tonight." He dutifully followed her lead to the elevator and her room.

When they reached her room, they took off their hiking boots and socks. Maeva took David's wrists in her hands and pulled him toward her. He noticed that both her hands and feet were beautiful but small for her stature.

After they had embraced and kissed deeply, Maeva reached behind David and pulled his T-shirt up and over his head and shoulders, letting it fall to the floor. She saw that he had dark hair on his chest, and she chuckled. "You have a little bit of bear on you." She ran her fingers and nails through his course chest hair while they kissed again.

David reached down and pulled her T-shirt over her head. Maeva's black wavy hair covered her face. She used both her hands to pull her hair back and, when she had completed that action, put both her hands behind her back and unfastened her sports bra. David lifted her breasts and caused her nipples to touch his. It was an almost electric sensation for him, and he noticed that her brownish purple nipples also stiffened in reaction.

She put her hands in the waistband of his hiking shorts and pulled him over by the bed. She pulled the bedspread off the queen bed and sat on the corner. She unfastened his shorts and pulled both his shorts and his underwear down to the floor. He was fully erect. She gently put her hands on his shaft and used her tongue to trace below the head of his penis. She felt him get even harder and his head enlarge.

She scooted back on the bed. David lay down next to her and put his hand on her thick wavy pubic patch. She was now moist with anticipation, and he gently massaged her clit. After he had brought her to near climax with his finger, he rolled on top of her.

She spread her thighs and placed her hands beneath each of her knees in anticipation.

As he started to glide inside her, she gasped and shuddered slightly. He then gave her his full length, and they made love slowly and intensely until he felt her shudder with orgasm. He followed quickly with his own. After a few moments, David started to roll onto his hip, but she draped her thigh over his and followed him with her strong leg so that he would not leave her. She held that position until she felt David go soft. Maeva lay back on the blanket and closed her eyes.

After a few minutes, Maeva felt David place his own thigh over both hers from behind. His long muscular arm nestled beneath her breasts, and he kissed the nape of her neck. She touched his arm and sighed. Although completely relaxed, her mind was going in many different directions. First of all, she would have to find a pharmacy tomorrow and use the Plan B formula. She knew that Colorado was a progressive state for female reproductive alternatives, and so Plan B was probably available over-the-counter.

Secondly, she would need to explore her contraceptive alternatives. Maeva had neither a gynecologist nor even a personal physician. She had full medical and dental insurance at Kingsley and Associates but had never wanted or needed a personal physician. Most of all, she would want a female doctor and one that was familiar with treating women with brown skin. A Pacific Islander doctor or physician's assistant would be difficult to find, but if she went to planned parenthood, the odds were that she could find a Black, Pakistani, or Indian practitioner.

These thoughts may have seemed premature, but Maeva felt a connection with this man that might well endure. She smiled as she sensed David's breathing becoming rhythmic.

Later that night, they pulled back the bedclothes and climbed naked beneath the sheets. David snuggled behind her, and they both fell into sleep. In the early morning hours, Maeva awoke to caresses along her stomach and thighs. She felt his erection grow in the small of her back. She turned toward him, kissed his lips softly, and rose to straddle him and guide him inside her.

CHAPTER 10

The next morning, they both awoke ravenously hungry. They had not eaten the night before. Fortunately, the Colorado Defense Lawyers Association provided an elaborate buffet breakfast for its members and guests. Maeva and David piled their plates. Maeva had mounds of scrambled eggs and fresh fruit. David had some of everything he could find and cups of fresh-brewed coffee. David enjoyed watching her eat. She was well-mannered but focused on her food. There was no idle conversation, and when she was finished with her plate, she returned to the buffet for more.

Sarah Spenser had seen the two of them enter the dining room. She had planned to approach David and start up some further conversation. However, as she observed Maeva and David, it was clear by their body language that they were a couple on this morning. When Maeva looked in her direction, Sarah quickly averted her eyes and addressed one of her table companions in animated conversation.

After breakfast, the two lovers were both in quiet contemplation. David eventually said, "I would love to stay and enjoy this beautiful Sunday morning with you, but I have to go rescue my boy,

Grady. His sitter has an absolute deadline of noon, and I'll have to get back."

Maeva replied slowly, "I did not realize that you had a son. Maybe I can meet him sometime."

"He is a furry son, half Airedale and half German shepherd according to the shelter where we got him in Castle Rock. The Denver Dumb Friend's League. Although, I suspect that the shelter just makes an educated guess on the breed. He was just ten weeks old when my late wife picked him out and brought him home. I would love for you to meet him. If you have time to drive out to Elizabeth this afternoon, we will just be hanging out."

"Yes, I heard about your wife's death. I'm so sorry." Maeva shook her head. "Unfortunately, and I do mean unfortunately, I have to meet Mr. Kingsley at 2:30 this afternoon and go over jury instructions for his trial on Monday. He makes closing arguments first thing in the morning, and the judge wants to see the final proposed instructions by 8:00 a.m. Otherwise, I would happily make the long drive to meet your furry son. May I reschedule?"

CHAPTER 11

W hen Maeva got to the office at approximately 2:00 p.m. that Sunday, Kingsley was already in his own office reading through the defendant's proposed jury instructions that Maeva had put in rough draft on Friday afternoon before leaving for the conference. When she looked into his office, he was just staring straight ahead, seemingly unfocused on the papers in front of him. He looked up to see her standing in the open office door and beckoned for her to come in and sit down.

"Maeva, you are a god-damned jewel to come in on a Sunday afternoon. I'm sure you had many better things to do, and I want you to know that I appreciate your efforts."

"It is all part of doing this type of work. You taught me that from the first day I ever worked here. Have you marked up the instructions for me to change?"

"I'm sorry, but I've just been looking at these papers and I have not been able to concentrate. My wife was hospitalized on Saturday with complications from her emphysema. I was at the hospital with her all day yesterday, and she seemed a little bit improved. She is one of those fragile ones struggling to breathe from an oxygen tank."

He glanced down and shook his head. "Maeva, honey, all I have had in my life is being a trial lawyer and then going home to my wife for all these years. As you know, we never had any children. It is dawning on me that I should have spent more time with her and less time in this office. Now she is in intensive care, and they severely limit the amount of time I can actually be in the room to be with her. Yesterday, I was so afraid that I was going to lose her."

Maeva could see the anguish and confusion in his face. He was always so calm and in control even in the most stressful situations. Now he was unashamedly wiping away tears that formed in his eyes. Maeva approached her boss and placed her hand on his shoulder. She said in a consoling tone, "I'm sure they're doing everything possible. If you want to go back to the hospital, I can get someone to help me prove the jury instructions this afternoon."

King said, "Thank you for the kind words. I am just going to focus on reading these new jury instructions for now." He rose and hugged her shoulders lightly.

Irving Roth had entered the room. He cleared his throat theatrically and said, "I came in to see if you two needed any help in trial preparation. Looks like Maeva is taking care of you. I will be here if you need me." Roth left King's private office and headed to his own.

They had major changes to make in the jury instructions. Their codefendant, a Denver hospital, had settled on Friday evening, paying out $6.5 million. King had advised his client, a manufacturer of hospital equipment, not to settle and to take the case to a final jury verdict. This was very risky because the plaintiff was the surviving daughter of a woman who died in a hospital incident.

The woman had died when she fell out of the bed which had been manufactured by Kingsley and Associates' client. The incident was unwitnessed, but the side rail of the hospital bed was down and the deceased patient was next to the bed. Photographs of the decedent showed a very elderly and frail patient who had apparently landed on her face and suffered a significant head and face injury.

The plaintiff's attorney's theory was that there was a design defect in the hospital bed, allowing the protective side rail to be up but not locked into position. Plaintiff's attorney's theory against the hospital was that the deceased patient had not been restrained and that the hospital personnel failed to check to see that the side rail was fully engaged and locked into position.

Now the attorneys and the judge were going to have to tailor the jury instructions and arguments solely on the theory that the hospital bed had a design defect, and that was a cause of the patient's death. It was a classic juxtaposition of a sympathetic individual versus a large corporation. Most jurors assume that the large corporation was either heavily insured or had enough assets that a wrongful death verdict could be easily absorbed.

King had worried throughout the trial that the jury might find both defendants liable based on sympathy and disparity of wealth. Now with the hospital no longer a defendant, the jury would be instructed that the hospital had settled out of the case but would not be informed about the size of the settlement. He felt much better about this scenario.

King tried to focus on the papers in front of him and keep his mind off his ailing wife. So far, he had not been successful, but his ability to compartmentalize and focus was legendary. His plan was to mark up the drafts with a red pen and let Maeva and Irving Roth put them in final form for presentation to the judge in the morning. Judges depended upon the attorneys to put the proposed instructions in final form so that there was no unnecessary delay for the jury panel.

The judge and the attorneys were well-aware that the jury instructions must be legally correct. The judge would read them to the jury before the attorneys made their closing arguments and a full packet of the jury instructions accompanied the jury into the deliberation room. Any deficiency or error in instructing the jury fully and properly could be the basis for a reversal of any jury verdict on appeal.

CHAPTER 12

David Richards pulled into his driveway and immediately recognized Marc Goodman's old Mercedes sedan parked in front of his garage. Marc was sitting in David's living room and watching a sports talk program discussing the Denver Broncos' preseason performance and what they would face in the regular season.

When David opened his front door, Grady bounded toward him, barking. As soon as he recognized his owner, he started moving in excited circles.

Goodman said, "I relieved Mrs. Dirksen of her pet-sitting duties about eleven o'clock this morning. I wanted to find out how the seminar went and also what may have transpired with Sarah Spenser. She told me that she was looking forward to being in Steamboat Springs with you."

"I'm sorry to report that Ms. Spenser was probably disappointed. The seminar went okay, but I'm sure that you could have given a more entertaining delivery. However, I am happy to report that Maeva Sopo was in attendance, and I got to know her better."

Goodman was clearly surprised. "Maeva, King's paralegal? She's the one that we met in Pueblo?"

"That's her."

"Wow, I'd always figured you for the petite blonde type. I mean, sort of like Jen. Sarah Spenser sort of fit that mold."

David did not reply. He sat down, pulled his cell phone from his pocket, and dashed off a text to Maeva. He told her that he hoped that she and King had good luck with the verdict and that he had spoken to Grady, who was very eager to meet her. He ended with:

dinner on Wednesday?

Within seconds, Maeva replied:

what time?

David smiled.

Goodman had been watching him and was also smiling. "I am guessing that you are going to see Maeva again soon. Good for you."

David changed into shorts and a T-shirt. He put on his running shoes and attached a leash to Grady. He told Goodman, "I know that you will help yourself to anything you want, but I will fix us lunch when I get back from my run."

Kingsley, Maeva, and Roth worked late on Sunday revising proposed jury instructions at their office. King also started to outline his closing argument on a yellow legal pad. It was the philosophy of Kingsley and Associates, PC, that the opening statement in a trial was much more important than a closing argument. Juries often tend to make initial subconscious assumptions based upon how well the attorneys' opening statement summarized what their evidence would show, and then filter the actual evidence presented to support their assumptions.

Given the fact that the hospital had settled out of the case and the jury would be aware of that fact, closing argument became more important than usual. King occupied himself with creating his closing argument and tried not to think of his wife, Kathy, in an intensive care ward.

On Monday morning, King was sitting at the counsel table with Maeva. Maeva was reviewing her exhibits to show to the jury during King's closing argument. She had all the exhibits loaded on her laptop and had been displaying them to the court and the jury at the appropriate times throughout the trial.

King had given her an outline of his closing argument, with handwritten stars where he wanted certain exhibits to be displayed during his final presentation. He had broken down his argument into two sections. The first would be on the issue of liability, or whether his client had produced a defectively designed product (the hospital bed in question), which caused the patient's injuries and death. The second section would be on the issue of damages sustained by the named plaintiff, the decedent's adult daughter.

The presiding judge was a senior substitute judge named Dorothy McGlaughlin. Judge McGlaughlin had a long career as a trial lawyer and had served on the bench as a Colorado district judge for fifteen years before taking senior status. Senior status meant that, although retired, a willing judge was available for temporary assignments.

Dorothy McGlaughlin had started when there were very few female personal-injury-trial lawyers. She was a little older than Kingsley, but he had tried cases against her when she was a lawyer. He had appeared before her when she was one of the best trial judges in Colorado. She had steel gray curly hair. She was thin and tall and quite self-assured. The trial judge who had been scheduled to preside over this wrongful death case was new to the bench, and he had never tried a civil jury case.

Given the complexity of the issues and the personalities involved, he requested that the chief judge assign a different trial judge due to his relative inexperience. The chief judge understood the situation and, rather than pick another judge in the district, decided to request Judge McGlaughlin, who had recently retired and was more than capable of handling the issues and the personalities.

The plaintiff's attorney was Roger Mortensen. Mortensen was forty years old and had a reputation of being an excellent trial attorney. He was blonde and had movie-star good looks. In front of the jury, he was deferential and respectful to Kingsley, but when there was no jury present, he was arrogant and condescending in his tone to every-one except for the judge and court staff. He considered himself to be the smartest person in any room and was buoyed by the fact that the hospital defendant had paid him $6.5 million on the preceding Friday. Now he had a major corporation as the remaining fat-target defendant.

Mortensen was even more confident in his position since Kingsley's client, a former member of the board of directors of the corporation, had admitted on the witness stand that later versions of the hospital bed in question had design changes to its side rails which enhanced patient safety. Although the corporate witness insisted that the subject hospital bed side railings were "safe," Mortensen had made the point that they were improved with later designs.

On that Monday morning, Mortensen made a tactical decision. He would argue only the liability of the corporate defendant in his initial closing argument presentation to the jury. He would reserve almost half his time for rebuttal argument and then stress the damage issues, outlining his justification for a large award of damages. In Colorado, the plaintiff is allowed to give an initial closing argument and then a rebuttal argument after the defendant's attorney responds because the plaintiff has the burden of proof in a civil case. The defendant has only one opportunity to give a closing argument.

Judge McGlaughlin seated the jury panel that Monday morning. There were eight members. Only six members would actually deliberate the fate of the defendant. Two extras were impaneled as alternates, in case of unexpected attrition, to prevent a mistrial. Barring exceptional circumstances, a civil trial was usually decided by six members. A stipulation to let all eight jurors deliberate was rare since the more jurors who deliberated, the greater the likelihood of disagreement.

After the jurors were seated, Judge McGlaughlin began to read the jury instructions, letting jurors know what law was to be applied and how to apply the legal concepts. She let them know that the arguments of counsel were not evidence and that the jurors were the ultimate fact finders. The judge always added her own personal comment that common sense was a valuable asset for each juror.

Maeva felt uncomfortable watching the plaintiff's attorney address the jury. He was glib and confident. He told them that the defendant's own corporate representative admitted that later versions of the hospital bed had safer side rails; that the corporation was aware that the prior design has been continued to be used in hospitals; and,

Mortensen argued, that the product posed a risk to every patient who had to undergo general anesthesia for a procedure. He argued that the hospital beds could have been retrofitted with the new safer bed rails, but that the corporate manufacturer was probably preoccupied with selling its manufacturing operations to China and reaping a huge profit.

Maeva watched King as Mortensen was taking these verbal shots at the corporate defendant. King showed no emotion and sat with his arms crossed in front of him. He did not take notes or react in the slightest. Maeva tried to do the same.

When the plaintiff's attorney had finished the initial part of his closing statement, he turned from the podium to King and invited him to respond. King turned to Maeva and winked at her. Only she noticed the gesture. King would never allow the jury to see him react.

King addressed Judge McGlaughlin before he walked over to the podium for his closing argument, "Your Honor, if it pleases the court, I would like to approach the bench on a legal point before I start my final presentation to the jury."

Judge McGlaughlin nodded her approval. Both attorneys and Maeva walked up to the judge's bench. Before anyone could speak, the judge flipped a switch so that her microphone was muted, and white noise was broadcasted to the jury so they could not hear anything said by the attorneys or the judge in the sidebar conference. A female court reporter was present to document the discussion.

A live court reporter, a human being, was one of Dorothy McGlaughlin's conditions to take on this case. She did not want a recording error to cause a mistrial or the basis for an appeal. Maeva asked permission to record the sidebar argument on her digital recorder, and the judge allowed her to do so.

"Your Honor, plaintiff's attorney, Mr. Mortensen, has elected to present only the issue of liability in his closing argument. He made no mention of damages. Should I elect to address only the liability issues, it is my understanding that Mr. Mortensen would be limited to true rebuttal and he would not be entitled to argue damages in any form to the jury panel. Am I correct in that assumption?"

Judge McGlaughlin looked at Mortensen for his position but stated, "Mr. Kingsley makes a correct point. You opted not to argue damages but stress liability issues. If Mr. Kingsley does not discuss damages in any form, the court is not going to permit any argument of damages to the jury in your rebuttal."

Mortensen was irate, and his face turned red. Although the jury could not hear his words, it was clear that he was angry with the judge's ruling. "This plaintiff is entitled to a presentation of her damage theories to this jury panel. To preclude my damage argument by this courtroom tactic is unconscionable."

Judge McGlaughlin did not react to his tone. She said in an even tone, "It appears to this court that plaintiff's attorney had opted to use a tactic where the defendant would not have an opportunity to rebut any damage argument. Whether that was calculated or a product of relative inexperience, you will be limited to only true rebuttal of any defense argument. That is the way it will be done. The jury instructions which were just read to the jury outlined damage concepts under Colorado law. Proceed, gentlemen." She leaned back in her chair and motioned for the attorneys and Maeva to return to their seats.

She smiled at the jury panel, turned on her microphone, turned off the white noise, and said, "The defendant now has an opportunity to present closing argument. The plaintiff's attorney, if he wishes, will have the final opportunity to respond to any argument made by the defendant. Members of the jury are reminded that the argument of counsel is not evidence."

Maeva sat down at counsel table. She was impressed with this tactical battle. King winked at her again and whispered, "I will not be needing any exhibits or technical presentations from the computer. We are going to do this the old-fashioned way."

Throughout the trial, the actual hospital bed had been present in the courtroom. Kingsley rose to his feet and, rather than approaching the podium, asked permission of the judge to approach the exhibit: the actual hospital bed. Judge McGlaughlin nodded and said, "Yes, of course, Mr. Kingsley. Feel free to interact with any of the admitted exhibits either in person or electronically."

Kingsley approached the hospital bed. The side guard rail had been left in the down position. He slowly raised the guard rail upward.

When it reached the fully vertical position to protect a patient, a loud audible click could be heard in the courtroom. The point was unmistakable. The old attorney looked toward the jury and said, "This is evidence. You will have every opportunity to examine this hospital bed and swing the guard rail up to this position. Each of you will note that it is extremely difficult, if not impossible, to put this side rail up without locking it into place." He paused for emphasis. "We all know what happened here. The patient was never restrained, and the guard rail was never raised to protect her. If either of those things had happened, the patient never would have fallen. It is that simple."

Kingsley walked over to the podium. "Thank you, members of the jury, for your patience and attention." Even though he was measured and controlled, it was obvious that he was full of emotion, and his voice changed subtly when he said, "I think we can all agree that this hospital bed would be put to better use for a patient in the hospital rather than as an exhibit in a courtroom." He said nothing further and walked back to defense counsel's table.

Plaintiff's counsel basically rehashed his liability argument for another half hour. At the conclusion of his remarks, he started to request a damage figure. Judge McGlaughlin watched King starting to rise from his chair for an objection. Instead of waiting for him to make a statement, the judge forcefully spoke over the plaintiff's attorney. The jury was distracted and surprised by Judge McGlaughlin's quick interjection and her disapproving tone. All they heard was, "Mr. Mortensen, we discussed this issue, and the court ruled. There will be no argument regarding damages from the plaintiff. Defense counsel never argued or even mentioned damages in his closing argument."

Mortensen turned red again and was clearly irritated by the judge's interruption. He abruptly walked over to plaintiff's counsel's table and took his client's hand in his. The plaintiff decedent's daughter was completely confused. The jury members were also confused but were left with the definite impression that the plaintiff's attorney had done something improper.

It took the jury less than an hour to return a verdict in favor of the defendant.

CHAPTER 13

David and Maeva were basking in the afterglow of having made love after dinner. Maeva pulled the bedclothes over her and David. The sheets on his king-sized bed were starting to feel cool. It may have been the wind howling outside on that autumn evening. David had cooked a chuck roast for them with roasted potatoes, green beans, and a Caesar salad. Maeva ate the meat and green beans but declined the potatoes and salad. She thanked him for the effort but reminded him that she rarely ate potatoes and severely restricted her carbohydrate intake.

"I certainly enjoyed the dessert," she said as she playfully bit his shoulder. She rubbed his chest hair and put her head where she had just rubbed.

Grady gave a low whine in response to hearing Maeva's voice. He was lying on the bedroom floor and had been dutifully silent up to that point.

Maeva let her arm dangle over the side of the bed. Grady approached and pushed her hand up with his nose. She gently scratched his muzzle.

"Can I ask you a question about our trial this week? I wanted to talk to King afterward, but he was preoccupied with getting back to his wife in the hospital. I suppose that I could have asked Irving Roth, but I'm not sure he would know. Did Judge McGlaughlin act improperly when she would not let Mortensen argue damages in his rebuttal argument and then interrupted him in front of the jury when he tried?"

David turned his head sideways to look her in the eyes. "I am not sure how I feel about you asking questions about the plaintiff's attorney right now. I remember you said you thought he looked a little bit like Brad Pitt. It's a little tough on my ego."

Maeva rolled her eyes. "Come on, be serious. It seemed like the rug was pulled out from under Mortensen at the last moment."

"I wouldn't feel too sorry for Mortensen. He did get $6.5 million from the other defendant. He should have known better. Especially with very experienced litigators like King and Dorothy McGlaughlin. He thought he was going to pull a fast one, and they called him on it. King did the right thing by approaching the bench and getting an advanced ruling. Judge McGlaughlin was just enforcing her own order, and it made Mortenson look terrible in front of the jury. Mortensen forced the situation. The jurors almost always look up to the judge, especially an older, soft-spoken, and mannerly judge like Dorothy. When she raises her voice and interrupts, it leaves quite the impression."

"Maybe I will get to see you and King in trial someday," Maeva said as she kissed David's neck.

"Not in the foreseeable future. The Kingsley firm is not on any of my personal injury cases, and it usually takes at least a year to get to trial from when the case is filed. Besides that, I prefer us as lovers rather than fighters." He held her closely. She was starting to nod off when David said, rather abruptly, "I've decided not to take any more new cases at the firm, and I'm going to start winding down my practice with the goal of retirement in a year or so."

"When did all this happen?"

"It's been coming on for a while, but I think I actually made this decision in the middle of my lecture at the seminar. I eventually want to move from this place and start a new chapter. My hope would be that we could come up with something that works for both of us, and Grady of course."

Maeva said nothing but gripped his hand fiercely. She had hoped that he was also thinking of a future together. She wanted to take him halfway across the world to Huahine and show him where she grew up. She wanted to show him to her friends and relatives on her home island. She thought he would like Huahine. It was green and warm and home. After they visited her island, they could start exploring the rest of the world and find a place that worked for both of them.

"And Grady of course," she said aloud.

The fall and winter found David and Maeva getting closer. It was busy for Maeva. King had two jury trials scheduled before the end of the year, which kept her and Roth occupied with trial preparation. King had told them that he thought both cases would not settle, so they were preparing for two ten-day jury trials in mid-November and the beginning of December.

David, on the other hand, expected none of his three scheduled cases to proceed to trial. Liability was not in question, and the damages were being negotiated in settlement discussions that, based upon his years of experience, would result in settlements. Defense counsel, in all three cases, had requested a settlement conference with the same professional mediator. Since the mediator had a reputation of getting even the most complex case resolved, David felt rather certain that the defense attorneys were preparing to settle rather than go to trial. King and David were both accurate in their predictions. However, both were also busy with trial preparation. Both knew that the surest way to lose a case or achieve a bad settlement outcome was to presume that the case was going to settle and not go to trial.

Despite the fact that both Maeva and David had a busy fall and winter, they found time to be together. This resulted in Maeva traveling to David's house and returning to Denver early the next morning. Although David had offered to meet her at her townhome in Greenwood Village, near both their offices, Maeva rarely wanted David to stay overnight in her place, or be there when she was not there. This was puzzling to David, but he acquiesced. He still worried when she had to drive the dark Elbert County roads with the large deer population.

The ten-day trial in November proceeded all the way to a verdict, as King predicted. Although Maeva was busy day and night during those ten days, David found time to attend two full days of the trial and show his support to King and Maeva. He had settled all his trials for the year and felt free to take some personal time off.

On the first day David showed up to observe the trial, he approached King and Maeva during a break. Maeva took David's hand and thanked him for coming to see her. King was confused at first but soon grasped the situation. He smiled broadly and shook David's hand, saying, "I am happy for you both. As I'm sure you know, she is a rare treasure, and you are a pretty decent guy yourself...for a plaintiff's attorney." King seemed genuinely pleased as he returned to his paperwork. Maeva kissed David on the cheek and returned to her computer on defense counsel's table.

King's trial in December unexpectedly settled. The plaintiffs, a family involved in a serious crash on Interstate 25, decided they did not want to proceed to trial, and their attorney accepted King's final offer. Since Maeva had only taken four days of vacation the entire year, King insisted that she take at least ten days off in December. The injured minor children in the car crash needed to have their settlements approved by the Denver probate court. King assured Maeva that Roth could handle the settlement approval hearings on his own without her preparation and support. She felt grateful and reluctant at the same time but accepted King's offer. She took the next week to finish up some projects and paperwork then headed out to Elizabeth to spend time with David.

Neither David nor Maeva were religious, but they were certainly feeling the Christmas spirit. They bought a real tree to decorate, stocked up on food and wine, and prepared to cocoon. It was fortunate they stocked up because a severe winter storm hit the prairie in Elbert County, and the area surrounding Elizabeth was blanketed in five to six feet of snow. Because the wind blew hard near

58

David's house, they had hardpacked drifts, some of which were seven or eight feet tall at the bottom of David's driveway.

Fortunately, they had nowhere to go and were in no hurry. David took his time clearing the driveway with a snow shovel and his snow-throwing machine. While he worked on the driveway in the mornings, Maeva would work out in the basement exercise area and use her laptop to keep up communications with the office. Grady would either run through the snow and the drifts, while David worked or curled up on the floor inside, watching Maeva. In the afternoons and evenings, they would prepare a meal, make love, nap, and watch movies. The snow and cold made it a guiltless isolation.

On the third day of snow removal, David got to the end of the driveway just when the Elbert County plows were blading his local road. David knew that it would take a few days for the county to get to his remote area and had been in no hurry to clean his driveway. Following the snowplow on his local road was an Elbert County sheriff's officer's four-wheel-drive Ford Explorer. The officer was the same officer who investigated Jen's fatal accident. He pulled over in David's driveway and said hello.

"It looks like you were able to not only dig out the driveway but, since you're still alive, you were apparently able to dig out around your furnace vents. Can't say that is true for some of your neighbors, especially the ones with older homes or elderly homeowners. We've had four bodies to collect from carbon monoxide poisoning." The sheriff's officer lightened the tone and pointed to the hills surrounding David's house. "Look at that blanket of snow. Must be still three feet deep in all directions. Won't last long when the sun comes out. It's beautiful when the sunlight hits it. Look at Pike's Peak, it's all covered with snow."

David glanced to the southwest and agreed that Pike's Peak was beautiful with its snowcap reflecting sunlight. The bright sun, the clear blue sky, and the deep snow cover in all directions made sunglasses necessary to see anything.

The sheriff's officer said, "All the main Elbert County roads have been cleared. Douglas County has cleared theirs too. It's a straight shot to Denver when you're ready. Probably won't be another one like this for the whole year, but you never know. Good luck." He raised the passenger side window and waved his goodbye. He started to follow the slow-moving snowplow, demonstrating that Elbert County was on the job.

Having finished clearing the long driveway and now having access to the local county roads, David went inside to share this information with Maeva. Grady met him at the door with his tail wagging. Maeva also met him at the door wearing nothing but one of his white T-shirts.

"I have good news and bad news. It's actually the same news," David said as he started to unzip his heavy Carhartt overalls. "The sheriff's officer says that all the roads from here to Denver are clear now."

"I do have mixed feelings about that development." Maeva came closer to him and unzipped the overalls the rest of the way to David's crotch. David pulled out of his heavy snow boots, and the Carhartt's fell to the floor. Maeva started to help him pull his heavy quilted sweatshirt over his head. David felt her nipples starting to harden as she pressed them against his now naked chest.

"I will go take a quick shower. Keep those thoughts."

"Oh no. I'm not waiting while you take a shower." Maeva kissed him and started to stroke his bare chest and neck. He could tell from her kiss, her voice, and the way she stroked him that she must have taken a cannabis edible. "In fact, I'm not going to wait another minute." She pulled the elastic band on his boxer shorts and reached down until she had his enlarging shaft in the palm of her hand. She led him into the bedroom by his elastic waistband. She pushed him onto the king-sized bed and stripped off his undershorts. She straddled him and lowered herself slowly but purposefully.

They both felt drained from their afternoon lovemaking and ended up taking an unplanned nap. Eventually, David began to hear Grady's soft whine, which was meant to inform his humans that he needed to go outside.

CHAPTER 14

T he next severe storm was a surge of COVID-19 infections and deaths. The news media had been covering the virus like it was a Chinese problem during January and February of the new year. It also become politicized in a presidential election year. Suspension of airline flights from China only confused the situation. By March, some people were wearing masks and gloves in the supermarket in Colorado. As befitting a divided nation, the populace was either becoming severely protective, or ignoring the virus completely. When the national and local economy started shutting down all but essential industries, COVID-19 was front and center on all the local newscasts and newspapers.

David and Maeva were used to being isolated together over the last several months. Now, David went into the town of Elizabeth one time per week to stock up on provisions. He wore a mask and gloves. He also scrubbed down all the grocery boxes and bags with a bleach mixture he had heard about on TV. The "experts" in the media seemed to be confused and divided about how the virus was spreading. Some seemed to think that surfaces should be sanitized, and others seem to believe that the virus was mainly airborne and that masks might prevent transmission.

When New York City seemed to be getting the worst of the transmission, David and Maeva were convinced that the virus must be an airborne disease since it appeared to be worse in close urban quarters. They continued to use their masks when out in public and indoors when not at home. Neither felt compelled to wear masks in the open air or while exercising in the country air.

All the state and local courtrooms went to Zoom calls for hearings. Live court appearances were rare, and masks and social distancing were the rule, as in most of the private economy. David's main floor home office space was set up for Maeva to use her screens and computers. David went up to his upstairs office area that was isolated from the rest of the house when he needed to communicate by Zoom or conference call.

Working from David's home was not a burden for either of them, but they both started to miss the interaction with their coworkers. Everyone had expected that the virus would be a short-term problem, but as winter turned into spring and summer, it appeared that business as usual and indoor restaurant dining was not going to be the new normal. Those businesses that could adapt to takeout, delivery, or online service survived. Grocery stores, liquor stores, and pharmacies soon emphasized online ordering and curbside pickup. The COVID-19 storm was shutting down the worldwide economy, as it had been known.

Maeva had been coming in to work at least twice a week since March. Although most of her colleagues and the Kingsley and Associates, PC, staff employees worked remotely by computer, Maeva was aware that King was not particularly computer-savvy. She came in to help with court filings, downloads of documents from opposing counsel and clients, and to make sure that King had everything he needed to stay current on his cases. She could field all his calls from either her townhouse or David's house, but she knew that he felt uncomfortable working solely by telephone.

She found handwritten memos on her desk from both King and Irving Roth. Roth came in the office about one time per week and left a few handwritten memos to Maeva or King to show that them that he had actually been in the office. Kingsley and all his employees wore masks whenever they entered the office building.

Much to Maeva's irritation, Roth got copies of all emails she sent and also had access to her billing records. She soon deduced that the Douche was billing the clients for reviewing all her work: either emails or the document she created in the office. Thus, he could watch her work, digest it, and keep current on his own billing through her efforts.

This was Irving Roth's paradise. He didn't have the stress of trials, hearings, or court appearances except by Zoom. Trials and routine court appearances seemed to be months away in the future, perhaps even being delayed until a viable vaccine for COVID-19 was publicly available for the general public. In the meantime, Roth would log his hours, enjoy his working from home, and depend on Maeva for all meaningful effort. It was a temporary luxury.

Despite the fact that King wore a mask and gloves everywhere he went and kept his invalid wife secluded at home, she caught COVID-19 in mid-May. Within a week, her weakened immune system gave out, and she was being kept alive on a respirator. It had only been eight days from the start of symptoms until she expired. King, of course, was crushed and unable to function for the rest of the month and beyond. The pandemic did not even allow for a proper funeral to be held because of the fear of contagion.

Maeva was able to cancel King's Zoom court appearances and reschedule discovery deadlines and telephone depositions. Most opposing counsel were sympathetic and eager to help in his grief recovery. Any deadlines or mandatory court filings were extended. In the rare circumstances where their opposing counsel was not cooperative, Irving Roth would schedule a Zoom hearing, or he or Maeva would just file a written motion explaining the circumstances.

Kingsley's reputation preceded him, and there was never a judge, magistrate, or clerk who did not automatically give a substantial extension of time to complete any projects. After all, very few jury trials were proceeding. Nobody wanted members of the public to be in close quarters at this stage of the pandemic.

The personal injury practice at Goodman and Richards, PC, was much the same. Everything proceeded by email, Zoom call, or in writing. By summer's end, they were going forward with depositions, court hearings, and settlement conferences through the Internet or telephone. New clients were being signed up with Zoom meetings. Thanks to modern technology, a new client could go from the initial Zoom client meeting to final settlement without ever stepping foot into their physical office. Their radio and TV advertisements stressed that Goodman and Richards, PC, was a safe and efficient avenue to pursue personal injury claims despite the worldwide pandemic.

David Richards rarely came into the office unless it was a very important meeting or business decision. He could speak to his clients or his office personnel from the comfort of his upstairs office. He had purchased a large monitor screen instead of relying on his laptop screen. Even though he watched Maeva going to work about two or three times per week, David had no desire to interact on an in-person level. He was able to help Goodman or their staff attorneys settle most cases from the comfort of his home office.

If they had difficult opposing counsel or an insurance company that was reluctant to pay what a case was worth, the Goodman and Richards, PC, law firm would merely set the case for trial and stop all communication. This was a tactic that worked very well with many of their cases where legal liability was not an issue, only damages. For instance, with a rear-end automobile accident. Defendants rarely won a rear-end automobile accident, and the main question for a jury was usually if and how badly a plaintiff was injured. Insurance companies were usually not willing to let a competent plaintiff's attorney have the opportunity to argue his or her client's damages to a jury if there were real and documented injuries. Settlement was always preferred to trial in uncertain cases.

Economically, the practice of law was moving ahead at the end of the first COVID-19 year for David Richards. His name was often used on firm pleadings with another attorney, but there was an in-house understanding that he was not intending to personally try any further cases other than those few remaining cases that he had personally started.

On September 1, Irving Roth and Maeva had been summoned to a rare in-person conference in Monroe County for a trial scheduled for the following January. Monroe County District Court was known for its palatial design and many courtrooms. It was an enormous structure and had a huge domed open entryway. Airport-like monitors had rolling scripts that would generally inform the public where certain legal proceedings were going to be held in the building. However, it was not business as usual in Monroe County. The crowds were small, and there were few in-person hearings and trials. Sheriff's officers had been positioned throughout the courthouse to enforce both a mask mandate by the Chief Judge and the required indoor social distancing.

Maeva and Roth were sitting in the open-air picnic area off the courthouse cafeteria. The cafeteria was closed due to the pandemic, but there were still vending machines that served soft drinks. Roth sat down at a concrete picnic table across from Maeva. He opened a can of Coke and set it on the concrete surface. He said, "Were you recording the judge when he outlined the pretrial motion deadlines and discovery cutoffs?"

"Yes. I'll put it in a memo form and prepare a schedule for both you and King."

"You and I are both going to be pretty busy if King is not going to be up to trying this case. He does not seem to be out of grief mode yet. The judge doesn't seem to be eager to continue any part of this case since the plaintiff is an elderly man, and he has already had one trial date postponed." Roth seemed to be talking to himself as well as Maeva.

"You want me to talk to King about getting another experienced trial attorney in the law firm to help out?" Maeva chose her words carefully. She did not want to convey the feeling that Roth might be over his head in a serious personal injury jury trial even though she believed that he might be.

Roth looked down at his can of Coke and said, "I am well-aware that King thinks that I'm only experienced enough to handle routine low-risk matters in court. But if you were to assure him and the client that you and I have everything scheduled and under control, they might not have a problem with giving me this opportunity to show what I can do. I know that both King and his clients have depended upon you for getting the cases ready for trial and respect your judgment. You have unusual personal clout for a paralegal, albeit one of the best-trained and highest-paid legal assistants in town." He drank from his Coke can. "I have always wondered how long it took for you to get so close to King and earn that *special* trust."

Maeva resented his tone. Here he was asking for her help and, at the same time, vaguely suggesting that there might be something else that explained her close professional relationship with King. She did not reply. She tried not to make eye contact with Roth because of her smoldering anger.

She looked down at his Coke can and noticed that a large yellowjacket wasp was walking around the rim of his red can. Roth had not noticed the insect while trying to make eye contact with Maeva. The yellowjacket crawled inside the Coke can and disappeared from sight. Roth raised the can to take another sip.

Just as the can was two inches from Roth's upper lip, the yellowjacket emerged and flew up right into his face. Roth screamed, and his high-pitched shriek echoed as it bounced off the six-storied walls surrounding the courtyard. The contents of the Coke can flew up as part of the surprised reaction and covered Roth's face, his cream-colored dress shirt, his expensive tie, and his khaki coat. He stood and was desperately trying to bat the yellowjacket from his face as the contents of the Coke can continued to slosh onto his front.

There were only two other people in the courtyard: two middle-aged women that were fifty feet away at another concrete picnic table. However, they both quickly figured out what had happened. One of the women pointed and started to laugh at Roth's flailing defensive antics. Maeva stifled a laugh but still had a smirk on her face when Roth recovered his composure and looked down at her. She produced a Kleenex from one of her coat pockets and held it toward him, still not speaking.

CHAPTER 15

Neither Roth nor Maeva had spoken since the yellow-jacket incident. They left the cafeteria courtyard and started walking down the halls of the Monroe County Justice Center toward the exit. They had both put on light-blue paper surgical masks as they moved indoors. It was late morning, and it appeared that most of the early court appearances were over. The hallways were almost deserted compared to pre-pandemic traffic.

Maeva was walking slightly ahead of Roth in the hallway. He reached out and placed his hand on her shoulder. She was genuinely surprised at this gesture and looked down at his hand. He said to her in a soft tone, "What I was trying to say to you was, I that hope that we can develop our own partnership and relationship." Maeva turned to face him and reply when his other hand moved down her lower back and cupped one of her buttocks.

"Don't you ever fucking touch me," Maeva screamed from behind her paper mask. At the same time, she shoved him with all the force she could muster, which was substantial. He careened backward into the nearest wall and collapsed, coming to rest in an involuntary seated position on his heels.

Maeva's loud reaction and the flurry of physical activity drew the attention of an African-American female sheriff's officer. The officer raced down the hallway and stood between Maeva and the still-seated Roth. She moved Maeva away with a firm hand on the paralegal's bicep. The officer realized that even though Maeva was wearing a mask, her black eyes were furious, and she might have continued to physically assault Roth without intervention.

Maeva looked down at the shorter, stouter sheriff's officer. They were making steady eye contact. Her nametag read: "Deputy Margot Baptiste." The officer had a close-cropped haircut. Her hair was salt-and-pepper. In a soft, even tone, the officer said, "I am not sure what is going on here, but a big strong girl like you cannot go around shoving a gentleman into courthouse walls."

Officer Baptiste turned her attention to Irving Roth, who was getting to his feet in the hallway. She observed that he was a dark-haired, handsome, well-dressed, and well-coiffed man in his early thirties. However, his shirt, tie, and coat were covered with a wet brown stain. She was truly puzzled about what must have transpired before Maeva's violent outburst.

"Are you okay, sir?" Margot Baptiste held up a hand when Roth started to approach Maeva.

"We are both fine," he replied. "Nothing to worry about, Officer."

"Just stay away from the lady for now." Officer Baptiste continued to hold her hand up, as if to restrain Roth from approaching Maeva. She turned to Maeva and said, "How about you, lady? Are we going to have some more physicality, or is this all over?" The sheriff's officer was treating the situation like she would a domestic violence incident.

Maeva had her arms folded across her chest and was considering her response. She eventually said, "It's all over for now. We will just be on our way."

"Well, I'm just going to escort you both out of the building to the parking area."

Maeva kept her distance from Roth as they exited the facility. Officer Margot Baptiste followed them out of the building, down the sidewalk, and into the parking lot. The three of them eventually arrived at Maeva's blue Mazda SUV. Maeva used her remote to unlock the doors. She got in the driver's seat, and Roth opened the passenger side door. The door was still open when Officer Baptiste looked across the interior of the vehicle and asked, "Y'all are going to travel together?" When Maeva reluctantly nodded her head, the sheriff's officer held up her hands and said, "All right, all right. Just be cool."

Neither spoke as they drove back to Denver. Maeva pulled up in front of their office building and stopped. Roth got out of her car without further comment.

Maeva drove straight to David's house in Elizabeth. She parked her car in front of David's garage and entered through the front door. Grady first barked and then greeted her with a wagging tail. David was working on a meal in the kitchen. Uncharacteristically, Maeva hugged David from behind and clung to him snugly. He sensed that something was wrong but waited for her to speak.

After a while, Maeva simply said, "That Irving Roth is a douche, just like they say. He thinks he's going to try King's upcoming cases for him to prove himself. He wants me to back him with King and the clients. That is not going to happen." She intentionally omitted any reference to Roth's groping attempt. David turned and embraced her.

"If King is still overcome with grief over his wife, you might mention the situation to Victor Beago. He is a seasoned litigator and will immediately know that Roth is not experienced enough to step in. However, my guess is that both King and Beago have contingency plans." He kissed Maeva, but she seemed distracted and preoccupied. She left the kitchen, and Grady followed her.

CHAPTER 16

King was in the office early the next morning. He wanted to get back up to speed on all his cases and was reviewing memos from Maeva and his attorneys. He had been the first person in the office. Maeva was the next. When she reached the threshold of his inner office, he looked up and motioned for her to come in. They were both wearing masks. She waited while King finished reviewing a memo. He seemed to be energetic and focused again.

King approached every case like it was his own personal mission. Just as he had years ago when he was a gunship helicopter pilot in Vietnam. Whether it was fifty years ago or the present, he was personally invested in the outcome of any undertaking and felt deep responsibility to achieve the correct final result. He insisted on detailed memos from all his employees so that he could look into any file and quickly determine whether a case was proceeding smoothly or required his intervention.

"Thanks for all your efforts while I was out of the office. Everything seems under control. I want you to know that this COVID business has made me rethink the state of the law firm, and

I'm going to make some changes. Some of these changes are going to affect you. Would you check the computer calendars for Vic Beago and Allison Brown? I want to set up a meeting with them in my office at the first available time for all of us. I want you to be there as well."

Maeva knew that these two attorneys, Beago and Brown, were Kingsley and Associates, PC's most successful and experienced associate trial attorneys. Both had complicated and challenging caseloads. They had also developed their own client base. If King had not compensated them so generously over the years, they would have moved on to form their own law firms. To keep them, he had paid them as if they were full partners.

Two hours later, King was addressing the three of them in his office. None of the three had any idea why they had been summoned. Neither Beago nor Brown had any court appearances that day. They were dressed casually to work in the office without any client contact. Allison Brown wore jeans and a green cotton sweater. Beago wore khakis and a polo shirt. Maeva had on a blue long-sleeved cotton shirt and gray slacks.

"Thank you for all your condolences in the recent past. I want you to know that some of the events have made me rethink the future of this law firm. I want to form a new corporation, and that corporation will be known as King, Beago and Brown, PC, if we can come to terms."

Both Victor Beago and Allison Brown looked at each other to determine whether either had anticipated this development. Both were genuinely surprised. Both were in their mid-forties and comfortable with their arrangement as top associate attorneys in the firm. Both were attractive, personable, and cautiously ambitious. Beago was of medium height and stocky build. He was swarthy and handsome. Allison Brown was a freckled redhead with a willowy figure. Both had a reputation of being professional, competent, and trustworthy.

King turned to Maeva and said, "Have you decided about going to law school? You know that you cannot be a shareholder in this law firm unless you have a law degree. The firm will pay for you to go to law school. The University of Denver has a program that will allow you to work while you're getting your degree."

Maeva looked at all three of the attorneys and said, "I'm good as King's paralegal for now."

"Your position in the new corporation will be litigation manager. You'll no longer be listed as just a paralegal in the new letterhead. You will remain as my number one assistant but also review all litigation in the firm on a weekly basis. We will be assigning you a new paralegal assistant so that you can delegate some of the ministerial details." He turned his attention to his attorneys. "To be part of the new corporation as shareholder partners, you will need to purchase at least one share of stock. I have 100 percent of the shares of the current professional corporation, and you may purchase as many as you'd like from me. That is, of course, if you are interested in my proposal."

Both attorneys nodded their assent. King continued, "I will have our accountant figure out the approximate net worth of the corporation so that each share can be assigned a value."

Allison Brown turned to Maeva and said, "We hope you choose the option to go to law school, but you'll have our full support whatever you choose."

CHAPTER 17

That evening, after the meeting at Kingsley and Associates, PC, Maeva went to her townhouse rather than traveling to Elizabeth. She called David and invited him to join her. He replied that he would take Grady for a run first and that both of them would be there soon. He promised to bring Thai food with him.

When they arrived, Maeva was sitting on her loveseat, sipping a glass of red wine. David could immediately tell that something was on her mind. He sat down in a chair opposite the loveseat and waited for her to speak. Grady rooted under her free hand, begging for a scratch. After she scratched behind his ears, Grady retreated to his usual place underneath the coffee table. Maeva related the events of the day.

In a slow and uncertain tone, David said, "Why don't you want to take up their offer and go to law school? With your brains and practical experience, you would be able to make it through easily and effortlessly."

"And be where? I am already being paid like an attorney, and now I will be overseeing everybody but King, Beago, and Brown. Maybe someday. It just does not feel right at this point in my life."

*****

The corporate change took place within weeks. The name change took place on the law firm entryway and the letterhead. Maeva was now the litigation manager, and no one questioned her new authority. Everyone already knew that King placed his full confidence in her abilities. The law firm threw a big formal catered announcement party, inviting clients and friends for food and drink in their office space.

Vic Beago, Allison Brown, and Maeva were the centers of attention at the party. King spoke and lauded his new partners and the anticipated bright future. David Richards attended but tried to stay in the background. All the associate Kingsley attorneys were dutifully attentive to the clients who attended. It was a strange party with the hosts and guests wearing masks and trying to be as socially distant as possible.

With the COVID pandemic still raging across the world, most Colorado courtrooms were still vacant. Routine hearings and court appearances continued to be held by audio or video teleconferencing unless the presiding judge insisted on personal appearances by the attorneys. Case preparation and settlement negotiations proceeded as normally as possible, either in the law offices or remotely from home.

Both Goodman and Richards, PC, and Kingsley, Beago, and Brown, PC, moved forward despite the coronavirus pandemic. David still rarely went to the office and preferred to work remotely on the few remaining cases where he was a consultant or the active litigator. Maeva now averaged three or four days a week in the office, trying to balance managing King's caseload with her new supervisory oversight.

It was after the US presidential election in November when King contracted COVID-19 despite all his efforts to isolate with masking and social distancing. It started with a cough, aching muscles, and flu-like symptoms. His doctor ordered quarantine and daily medical teleconferencing to monitor his symptoms.

When King's symptoms worsened and he had more difficulty breathing, he was hospitalized. Maeva had been visiting King by Zoom meeting the first two days of his quarantine. Thereafter, he was always unavailable for Zoom or telephone. She and David went to the hospital to visit King but were not surprised when they were denied personal access. The attending nurse advised them, through a glass partition in the waiting room, that no patients could have visitors. She looked at King's chart and discovered that there was a medical power of attorney, naming Maeva as the person who could make medical decisions on behalf of King if he was not able to do so.

Out of David's earshot, the nurse whispered in Maeva's ear that King was on a ventilator and would be in an induced coma, pending respiratory stabilization. She took all of Maeva's contact information. Maeva made certain that the hospital also had David's contact numbers in case of emergency.

Maeva never had to make any decisions on King's behalf. He died on the sixth day of hospitalization without regaining consciousness. All she had to do was okay the transport of his remains to the funeral home for cremation. The ashes would be held until such time as a memorial service could be held at the funeral home. When it would be allowed was unknown. It seemed so bizarre that she never had the opportunity to personally say goodbye when he was ill.

CHAPTER 18

Kingsley, Beago, and Brown, PC, issued a pleading known as a Suggestion of Death in all court cases where King had been the principal counsel. Maeva also prepared an entry of appearance pleading for Vic Beago in all cases that had been set for trial. Irving Roth was still listed as a secondary counsel. Maeva personally telephoned every client or corporate representative to assure them that their cases were being given all appropriate attention in the wake of King's death. It was still an uncertain time.

Beago and Roth were summoned to appear in Judge Samuel Donaldson's courtroom in Monroe County district court to discuss the status of a personal injury jury trial scheduled the following month after King's death. Maeva also accompanied the two attorneys. The opposing plaintiff's counsel objected to any delay or continuance of the scheduled jury trial on the grounds that the plaintiff's health was uncertain. The status conference took place in open court because the judge and the attorneys could socially distance themselves in a large courtroom, as opposed to the judge's chambers, where these types of proceedings usually took place in normal times.

After counsel had introduced themselves, Judge Donaldson indicated that the proceedings were going to be recorded electronically. Maeva requested and was granted the ability to use her own digital recorder. Declining any formal statements, Judge Donaldson indicated that he was aware that the plaintiff had prostate cancer. The plaintiff, in his early sixties, was named Jeremiah Dawson.

Judge Donaldson had reviewed the pleadings filed and indicated that he had to balance the interests of the plaintiff's health with the disadvantage to the defendant in having a lead defense lawyer die within a month of trial. He noted that Mr. Beago was an experienced and able trial attorney and that Irving Roth had been secondary counsel from the outset of the case. However, the judge thought that the defense would be put in a very unfair position to proceed to trial so soon.

Judge Donaldson also emphasized that Victor Beago had candidly represented to the court that Irving Roth was not ready to be lead counsel in a case with this large a monetary exposure. He granted a postponement of the trial for ninety days only. He noted that the plaintiff's prostate cancer had been diagnosed for quite some time, and it was a slow-moving and a controlled illness. He ordered that this case be given priority and that any conflicting cases on his courtroom docket would be given secondary status. He proceeded to set forth the date for the new jury trial to proceed for up to two weeks. No further postponements would be allowed, and he set forth specific deadlines for any pretrial matters to be concluded without exception.

Maeva glanced at Roth and saw that he was red-faced and furious with the judge's comments about his inexperience. She remembered that he wanted this opportunity to prove himself as a capable trial attorney.

After he had finished ruling, Judge Donaldson asked, "Are there any unanswered questions?"

Plaintiff Dawson's attorney, a burly gray-haired and bearded man, rose and addressed the judge in a whiny voice, "Judge, I have another matter scheduled on the date of the new proposed trial."

"Whatever it may be, tell them that you now have an expedited and emergency trial date in my courtroom that cannot be continued. Any other questions or comments from either side?" Judge Donaldson's tone made it clear that he was not going to reconsider any part of his order. When neither side said anything further, he said, "That will be all. Court is adjourned." He walked off the bench.

Vic Beago, Irving Roth, and Maeva Sopo left the courtroom and walked down the hallway of the Monroe County judicial building. When the three of them reached an empty courtroom, Beago opened the door to a small adjacent counsel's conference room and motioned them inside. He turned to Maeva and said, "We need to set up an internal schedule and decide who is going to be responsible for each step. Did you get everything that Donaldson said?"

Maeva nodded, reached into her shoulder bag, seemed to rearrange its contents, and pulled out a yellow legal pad and a pen, expecting Beago to discuss the schedule and assign responsibilities. Instead he looked at his watch and said, "I have another hearing on a case of my own in Denver district court in less than an hour. I have to run. Why don't you two discuss a preliminary schedule, and I'll look it over later." He rose and left the conference room, closing the door.

Maeva did not want to be alone in the conference room with Roth. She started to stand to leave. Roth surprisingly said loudly, "We are not done yet." He put his hand on her shoulder to keep her from standing. "I know you're the litigation manager now, but you're still just a fucking paralegal and I am an attorney. I'll let you know when we are done here."

Maeva stood defiantly erect despite Roth's pressure on her shoulder. She said, "I am done." As she started to collect her legal pad and pen from the small conference table, Roth suddenly struck her temple with his closed fist. She saw stars and collapsed. Roth caught her before she fell to the floor and placed her face down on the conference table. Maeva was motionless and unresponsive. Roth spat out, "You haughty bitch," to her unconscious form.

As Maeva started to regain consciousness, she felt her pantyhose being peeled down her thighs as she was prone on the small conference table. Her skirt had been hiked up above her waist. She screamed, "God, no! Leave me alone, you asshole!"

78

"Scream all you want. This is a soundproof conference room, and there's damn few people in the hallways. Just relax and take it." The sound of his belt and pants hitting the floor filled the small conference room.

Maeva saw her pen and legal pad on the conference table edge. She grabbed the pen, twisted her torso on the conference table, and stabbed Roth in the cheek below his eye. Roth took her face and slammed it into the conference table in response. Although she had barely regained consciousness, Maeva realized that this is when she had to act. She swiveled and sat to face Roth again and jammed the sole of her foot toward his groin with all the force she could muster.

He had anticipated her kick and started to retreat, making the blow ineffective. He pounced upon her again and slammed her head and shoulder into the conference table. She was still dazed but felt him trying to spread her thighs. She twisted again with the pen in her hand, and this time the pen found Roth's earhole. Roth's eyes opened wide. Maeva successfully kicked him away from the conference table and stood up.

The room started to spin for Roth. His inner ear had been pierced, and his equilibrium was completely off. He struggled to stand upright and pitched slowly to his left, unable to break his fall. His face, with the pen protruding from his ear, hit the conference room floor, and the pen slammed into his brain with its remaining length. Roth swiped at his ear, but the pen had penetrated its complete length. His body started to spasm, and the blood started to flow from the punctured inner ear.

Maeva sprang to the conference room door, opened it, and screamed down the hallway: "Please! Help us. Someone, help us. Please help!" She pulled up her pantyhose and pulled her skirt down. Her screams echoed down the hallway, and she soon heard footsteps on the stone floors.

Sheriff's Officer Margot Baptiste was the first to arrive. She recognized Maeva from their prior encounter weeks ago. She looked into the conference room and saw Roth's body spasming and blood flowing onto the floor. Baptiste noted that Maeva's demeanor was neither threatening nor violent. Baptiste was unsure what to do. She decided to radio for assistance.

In the interim, she took out her handcuffs and clicked them on Maeva's wrists behind her back. Maeva was confused but said nothing. In less than a minute, there were several sheriff's deputies on the scene. They isolated Maeva along the hallway corridor, while the ranking deputy called for an ambulance. Roth's form had quit spasming, but his blood kept slowly pooling along the conference room floor.

Baptiste put her face right in front of Maeva's and said, "I know you're an attorney, but I have to read you your Miranda rights before you say anything."

"I am not an attorney. I'm a paralegal. You need to know that I am the victim here."

"You may be. That is going to be for the district attorney to decide. That gentleman is either dead or dying." Baptiste slowly escorted Maeva down the hall toward the sheriff's holding cells in the Monroe County Judicial Center.

CHAPTER 19

Maeva's first telephone call was to David's cell phone. He answered and listened to Maeva's confusing, halting speech. She said Irving Roth was dead and that she was being held in the Monroe County sheriff's courthouse jail. David could not comprehend what was going on and asked that she give the phone to a sheriff's officer. Maeva passed the phone to Officer Baptiste. Baptiste was professional and brief. She said that Maeva was apparently involved in or witnessed a homicide. She would not respond to David's many questions other than to say that she would probably need a lawyer. She told David that Maeva would be transported to the Monroe County sheriff's main office pending review of the case by the district attorney.

David was immediately on the phone to Marc Goodman. Both of them had been district attorneys in their remote past and realized that a homicide was nothing to be taken lightly. Despite only handling civil matters at that time, Goodman still had many friends who practiced criminal law. Goodman said he would make a few phone calls and call David back. In the meantime, David said he was driving to the Monroe County Judicial Center to see if he could see Maeva.

When David reached the sheriff's office, he was asked for his Colorado Bar Association card. When David explained that Maeva was his girlfriend, the duty officer indicated that she would only be able to speak with her attorney of record for the time being. Frustrated, David sat down in the waiting room. He called Goodman on his cell phone and was told that help was on the way.

Marc Goodman showed up in less than an hour in the company of a short Hispanic woman in her mid-thirties. The woman was immaculately dressed in business attire. She was introduced to David as Patricia Archuleta. She was polite and pleasant to David but all business. Despite her small stature, she filled the room with her presence. She approached the duty officer and said, "I represent Maeva Sopo, and I want to see her right now." She handed him her bar card and stared at him impatiently.

The duty officer picked up a telephone and indicated that Maeva Sopo's attorney was here to see her. David rose to follow Attorney Archuleta when the sheriff's officer escorted her to a jail meeting room. The deputy stopped him and said only her attorney would be permitted to speak to her at the present time. He was told that he could wait for visiting hours.

David looked completely puzzled when he turned to Goodman. He said, "I recognize Patricia Archuleta from television. How does she fit in? What the hell is going on?"

"When I heard that there were potential homicide charges, I called Patricia immediately," Goodman spoke in his usual soft and controlled manner. "There is no better attorney in the state. Do you remember that case involving a Denver Bronco defensive lineman that was accused of rape? She not only successfully took the case to a jury but she got a verdict of acquittal within twenty minutes of jury deliberation and then sued the county for bringing charges in the first place."

David remembered the vision of the tiny defense lawyer standing next to a 320-pound lineman in court. He remembered been impressed about how she filled the courtroom with her personality. Even on television, her courtroom demeanor was impressive.

The law partners waited in the lobby of the sheriff's office for approximately an hour. Patricia Archuleta eventually was escorted to the waiting room and joined them. Archuleta was relaxed and made direct eye contact with David. "I understand that Maeva is your significant other and Marc is your law partner. Marc and his wife, Ruth, are good friends. Ruth is teaching me mah-jongg. I am the only Mexican in their group. I know that you were a district attorney in your past life, so I want you and Marc to enter your appearances in this case as Maeva's legal counsel. Eventually, the district attorney is going to object and name you as a potential witness. Until then, you can enjoy the ability to meet with her, and your communications will be shielded under the attorney-client privilege. We will see how long that lasts. Marc should be able to serve as my cocounsel even if this case proceeds to trial." She paused her lawyer speak and said to both men, "She would rather be alone this evening."

David looked at her with a dumbfounded stare and said, "What the hell is going on, Ms. Archuleta? Why is she being treated as a suspect, and how did the death happen?"

"I want you to know that I'm going to charge only a fraction of my usual hourly rate. I usually get $750 per hour on a homicide case. You and Goodman are getting the friends-and-family rate." She motioned David and Marc outside the sheriff's office. They both followed her into the parking lot. She looked over her shoulder and then spoke in a level tone. "Ms. Sopo appears to have been the victim of an attempted rape. She acted appropriately and defended herself. The attacker died from wounds which Ms. Sopo inflicted in her defense. I have made arrangements to meet with the district attorney tomorrow morning. I know him from our law school days. I want to review their evidence and discuss the proposed charges. The meeting is at 10:00 a.m. If you both could file your entries of appearance on this case first thing in the morning, Mr. Richards can join me at the meeting with the prosecutor."

"When can I see her?" was the only question David could muster.

"Once you are an attorney of record, we should be able to make arrangements for you to see Maeva after our meeting with the district attorney." Patricia Archuleta held out her hand to shake David's and then Marc's. "I will see you tomorrow." She left without further comment. There was no question about who would be in charge.

David put his hand on Marc Goodman's shoulder in a gesture of thanks. They both nodded in their appreciation of the situation.

CHAPTER 20

A t 10:00 a.m., Patricia Archuleta, David Richards, and a young district attorney by the name of Mitchell Wild were sitting in a conference room in the offices of the Monroe County District Attorney. Patricia was both irritated and amused that they would send a "baby" assistant DA to meet with her.

Wild appeared to be in his mid-twenties. He had a fashionable short blonde haircut, white dress shirt, and royal blue tie. All three attorneys were wearing gloves and paper gowns to prevent contamination of the physical evidence. In addition to the clothing worn by Irving Roth and Maeva Sopo, there was Roth's briefcase, the satchel shoulder bag worn by Maeva, and the respective contents of both separated but strewn all across a conference table covered with butcher paper.

All three attorneys were standing by the conference table, looking down at the physical evidence, when Mitchell Wild said, "Everything's here except for the pen, which is still in Dworkin's ear and brain. The coroner will be holding onto that until the formal autopsy has been completed. Ms. Sopo has been examined. The examination confirmed her statement that there was no penetration involved. No semen or other evidence of sexual conduct was discovered. As I'm sure you are aware, Ms. Sopo has a large bruise on the side of her face and temple. Mr. Roth had a stab wound below his eye on his left cheek, probably from the first jab of the pen. There was no torn clothing. The only blood appears to have come from the decedent's ear canal." Wilde was reading from notes on a clipboard.

After looking at the array of physical evidence, Patricia Archuleta picked up Maeva's digital recorder. The young DA was carefully looking over her shoulder as she examined the recorder with her gloved hand. She tried to turn it on and soon discovered it had no charge. She opened the back of the recorder and held it up for David to view. "It takes two AAA batteries. I will help you take off your gown and gloves. Would you see if you can find some batteries so we can turn this thing on?"

"No need for that." Wild picked up a telephone receiver and asked the person on the other end to bring two AAA batteries to the conference room. He watched Patricia Archuleta look over the displayed physical evidence. She continued to hold onto the digital recorder. Within minutes, a young female employee opened the conference door and handed Wild the requested batteries.

Archuleta handed the recorder to David while she continued her visual inspection of what lay before her. David put the batteries in the recorder, after putting a fresh pair of gloves on, and checked to see if it would operate. Archuleta took the recorder from him, turned up the volume as high as possible, placed it on the conference table, and started the playback.

The first recorded item was Judge Donaldson outlining the terms of a continued trial date, including deadlines for pretrial motions and supplemental expert disclosure documents. After clicks and pauses, the digital recorder started to playback again with Vic Beago's deep baritone voice requesting that Maeva and Irving Roth work on the trial scheduling and deadlines. Beago excused himself to travel to another appointment, and they could hear a door opening and closing. The recording continued to playback with all the conversation, the smack of Roth's fist hitting Maeva's face, the struggle, the screams, the sound of Roth's body hitting the floor, the conference door opening, and Maeva's final scream for help. Once they heard Baptiste's and the other sheriff's officers' voices, Archuleta turned off the recorder and stared directly at DA Wild.

"This recording completely confirms my client's contention that this was an attempted rape and justified self-defense to a physical assault. No further investigation needs to take place other than to get your boss to listen to this recording. I will assume that you do not have the personal authority to conclude the DA's investigation. The Monroe County District Attorney's Office has until 4:00 p.m. today to release Maeva Sopo from custody and issue a statement that she was the victim of a brutal physical assault and not a suspect nor a person of interest in the homicide death of Irving Roth. If she is not released, Mr. Richards's law firm will file a civil lawsuit against the district attorney's office, the district attorney himself, you personally, the Monroe County Sheriff's Department, and all the individual sheriff's officers, alleging false arrest, false imprisonment, violations of Ms. Sopo's civil rights, and what other claims they deem appropriate."

She handed the digital recorder to the young DA. "Do it now. You and your boss call my office this afternoon to confirm that all my demands will be honored. Now both Mr. Richards and I would like to see our mutual client without further delay."

*****

Within minutes, Maeva was escorted into the conference room by a female sheriff's officer and Mitchell Wild. Wild was still holding the digital recorder. Maeva was not physically restrained. Both Wild and the sheriff's officer left the conference room and told them that they had the use of the conference room for as long as they wanted it.

David strode past Archuleta and hugged Maeva. She looked up at him, and he could tell that she had been crying. Her eyes were bloodshot, and her eyelids and cheeks were puffy. Blood filled the corner of the white of her eye near the bruised temple. He said, "We're going to try to have you out of here this afternoon."

Archuleta corrected him by saying, "No. You will be out of here this afternoon. This is all bullshit." She explained that they found her recorder and everything that happened in the conference room had been documented. "Exactly like you described it to me."

David hugged Maeva and kissed her on the cheek. She placed her hand on his face and said, "I'm sorry, baby. I have made a mess of things." She buried her face in her hands and sobbed silently.

Both David and Patricia Archuleta said simultaneously, "You have nothing to be sorry about."

Archuleta continued, "You are the victim here. That bastard forced your hand. Most women wouldn't have been physically and mentally able to do what you did. Thank God that recorder was on and got the whole thing."

Maeva began to quietly sob again. They escorted her to a chair, and Archuleta left the room to give the lovers some privacy. Archuleta called her office on her cell phone and made arrangements to have some replacement clothing brought for Maeva. She made an educated guess on the sizes. Maeva should never have to see the evidence clothing again.

The DA released her by 2:00 p.m. with a written apology for her detention and condolences for her being a victim of a violent crime. David remained with her until her release. He offered her a choice of wearing her own clothes, or the sweats that Patricia Archuleta had arranged for her. She opted for the new sweat clothes. Patricia had guessed accurately for the sweat clothes, but the slip-on canvas shoes were much too big. Maeva's hands and feet were smaller than one might have expected, given her stature and build. She slipped on her own shoes to depart the Monroe County Judicial Center.

She was quiet during their hour drive to David's house in Elizabeth. David was worried about her mental state but did not press her with any questions or comments.

When they arrived, Grady was happy to see them. He'd been in the house for several hours but had to greet and interact with Maeva before he went outside. David and Maeva went outside to sit at the wrought iron table on David's concrete porch. It was mid-November but warm. However, his backyard was no longer green and full of summer life. The butterfly bushes and sunflowers that lined the retaining wall staircase planters were brown and dried. The lawn and field were also lifeless and dormant. The hummingbirds, goldfinches, and other birds of summer had long departed.

Off to the west, the line of cottonwoods along the distant stream that flowed through the middle of his cattle ranch neighbor's place had lost their leaves. Even though it was mid-November, no snow had yet fallen, and the temperatures were unusually warm for this time of the season. David went to the kitchen and returned with two Dale's Pale Ale blue cans. David opened his and drank deeply. Maeva was uninterested. David asked, "Is there something else you want?"

Maeva shook her head and looked off into the western sky.

"I am not sure that I can ever go back to my office. No matter what the circumstances, I killed a coworker. King is dead. Everything has changed now."

"It is way too soon to make any decisions. Sleep and reflect." David squeezed her hand. Grady came up on the porch and rooted his muzzle underneath their clasped hands. Maeva smiled and reached down to hug Grady with the crook of her elbow. Maeva and David went to bed early that night without much more conversation. In the early morning hours, Maeva snuggled up to David, and they eventually made love slowly and gently. Both fell back to sleep in the quiet darkness.

CHAPTER 21

Maeva was up early the next morning. She was dressed in jeans and wore one of David's fresh long-sleeved dress shirts. There were many to choose from since he was no longer going into the office or routinely appearing in court. The sweat clothes she had been given merely reminded her of the ordeal she had endured. She patiently waited for David to arise and drink some of the coffee that she had made. She asked him to take her home when he was ready.

"Are you sure you should be alone right now? There's no reason we can't hang out here today or forever until it feels right."

"No. I need some alone time to sort this all out and figure out where I'm going."

David drove her into Denver late in the morning and walked her to her door. She promised that she would call him if there was anything she needed. David was confused but gave her her space.

Patricia Archuleta's office was only blocks away in the Denver Technological Center. He parked in the spacious parking lot and went up to her office, hoping she would be there. Luck was with him. The receptionist showed him to her large and luxurious individual office where she was reading a file on her desk. She looked up at David, leaned back in her office chair, and said, "I am sure that you are here to take me to lunch and buy me some top-shelf tequila. Nothing is on my afternoon calendar, and I am hungry and thirsty. I know just the place."

The upscale Mexican restaurant and tequila bar was quiet and subdued on a weekday. They were escorted to an outside table on a patio since indoor dining had been eliminated by pandemic executive orders. There was only takeout and outside dining in the Denver metropolitan area. Fortunately, it was another unseasonably warm late-November day. Patricia ordered both the drinks and the lunch for them. She said, "You have to trust a Mexican who would take you to a Mexican eatery."

The tequila came first. Patricia drank deeply from a double shot glass and bit down on a wedge of lime that had been served on a small plate. David sipped his glass.

"How is Maeva?" Patricia's tone was serious.

"Subdued and sure that all this has changed her life forever. She doesn't think she can go back to the law firm and face her coworkers."

Patricia finished her tequila and motioned to the waiter for another. She put both her hands flat on the table in front of David and leaned forward to emphasize her words: "I do not know Maeva as well as you do. However, I know that she is a strong, capable woman who was used to being in control of her world. An attempted rape, even a failed attempt, is an assault on her independence and sense of self. You and I both know that rape is not a sexual crime: it's a need for the perpetrator to physically conquer and control the victim. That man was threatened by Maeva's competence and self-assurance. He acted out in an attempt to claim some twisted image of his own self-importance."

She continued to stare at David to see if he understood her words. Her black hair framed her face, and he could feel the power of her personality. She drank more of her tequila and sat back in her chair, waiting for David's reaction.

"I understand and appreciate what you are saying, Patricia. I just don't know how hard to encourage her to get back with her career."

Patricia raised her hands dramatically over her head. "Who knows? She needs to be in control of her life now." She leaned forward again. "Maybe she goes back to work tomorrow, or maybe she never goes back to that office at all. Just support whatever decision she makes and don't second-guess her. Give her time, David."

Their pork tamales and chili rellenos were placed before them on sizzling plates.

"It is just kind of a goddamned shame that a tall, dark, handsome, and sweet guy like you is already taken." They both smiled, drank their tequila, and enjoyed their lunch.

CHAPTER 22

After lunch with Patricia Archuleta, David drove back to Maeva's townhome to check on her. Her Mazda SUV was not in the parking space. He used his key and went inside. She was gone, but there was a note on her kitchen counter that said: "Taking care of a few things. Talk to you later. I love you. M."

David drove back to Elizabeth. On one hand, he was happy that Maeva seemed to be taking control of her life. On the other hand, he thought that she definitely needed more rest from her ordeal. Of course, rest and nonaction was not in her character. He just hoped that she was in a healing phase.

It was such a warm and sunny November afternoon that David decided to take Grady for a long run. They ran down to the conservation easement by the Spring Valley Ranch creek. After that, David led them down a dirt road in undeveloped hilly ranchland. It felt good to run on a dirt surface in the clean country air. On the way back, he stopped to let Grady sniff and explore rather than just heeling and following his run. David took his time on the way back, letting Grady explore every interesting bush and smell.

When they got home, David tried to sit down and work on another speech that Marc Goodman wanted him to give to a group of insurance adjusters. He stared at a blank laptop screen for a while. When he could not compose, he took a shower and dressed. Maeva was foremost on his mind, and he could not concentrate on a stupid speech despite the outline Goodman had provided for him.

He decided to call Goodman and let him know what had transpired at the Monroe County DA's office. David expressed his appreciation at Goodman hooking them up with Patricia Archuleta.

"Isn't she amazing?" Goodman was genuinely impressed with Archuleta. "She earns and gains more respect in every room she enters."

Goodman listened patiently while David told him about how concerned he was about Maeva. She sounded and acted appropriately, but she was clearly, to David's observation, not the same woman she had been prior to the attack. Something shut down and she was moving, but David wasn't sure where she was heading.

Goodman chose his words carefully for his friend and law partner. "It is not every day that you are forced to kill someone in self-defense. How can you be the same person you were before that happened? Maeva is mentally and emotionally strong. Your relationship is strong. You need to let her fly where she's going to fly until she decides to perch again. In a sense, she is like you were after Jen's death." Goodman paused then began again. "We knew you were the same David Richards, but we were not sure how you would see the world you lived in."

David thanked Marc and told him that he would see him soon.

David called Maeva's cell phone. There was no answer, so he left a message asking her to let him know when he could see her again. He told her he loved her and would wait for her. David browned a pound of ground turkey. He took out half and saved it for a topping for Grady's kibble meal that night and the next two nights. He added some chili beans to the remainder of the meat in the skillet and ate that for dinner along with some fresh flour tortillas and two Dale's Pale Ales. He was asleep in front of the TV by eight o'clock that night. He eventually woke up about midnight, let Grady out in the backyard for a final tour, and then they both went to bed and slept until seven the next morning.

David immediately checked his cell phone the next morning. There were no messages from anyone. He made some coffee and then decided to work out in his downstairs exercise room. He brought his cell phone with him in case Maeva might call. After his workout, David tried to work on his speech again but was still unable to concentrate.

David drove into the Denver offices of Goodman and Richards, PC. Even fewer employees and attorneys were in the office than the week before. Apparently, working remotely was how the law firm was coping with the COVID pandemic. He sat in his office and looked at the mail in his inbox that had accumulated. He returned the pile of mail to his paralegal's office for scanning and filing in the appropriate electronic folders.

David left his office, got in his Chevy Tahoe, and drove by Maeva's townhouse. Her Mazda SUV was not in the parking slot. He decided to drive the few blocks to the Kingsley law firm parking lot. Even though he did not see the Mazda in the parking area, he parked the Tahoe and decided to go up to their offices. A petite female African American receptionist told him, through her paper surgical mask, that Maeva was not in the office but that she was sure Vic Beago would want to talk to him. She got on the office intercom and spoke briefly with Beago. She led him back to Beago's individual office (which happened to be Kingsley's former office suite).

Vic Beago rose from his desk and walked over to shake David's hand. "Dave, I was meaning to call you. I'm sorry that you had to make the first move to talk about this Maeva business." His rich booming voice tried to be reassuring. He looked up to David's face and gave him a somber smile.

"Have you seen her, Vic?"

"Yes, yes. She was in this morning. She let us know that she needs to take an indefinite leave of absence. She said she was going home. I wasn't sure what she meant by that. I told her that we had some firm business to discuss with regard to Kingsley's death, his stock ownership, and some other matters. She didn't want to discuss anything this morning, and I respected her wishes. I could tell that she was distraught in her own controlled way. She told me that she would be back in touch with me at the right time."

David thanked him and turned to leave. He was walking down the hallway toward the glass entryway to the Kingsley law firm when the petite Black receptionist stood and held up a hand. She said, "I'm Lynette. I know that you don't know me, but I was fairly friendly with Maeva. You know, office friends. I tried to talk to her this morning, but she was having none of it. She told me she had to sell some things, and she was in a hurry. She gave me her firm cell phone." Lynette stepped back behind the receptionist desk and held up the cell phone, as if to prove her credibility. "I wanted you to know in case you try to call her on that number."

He thanked her.

David hurriedly left the parking lot and drove back to Maeva's townhouse. He had to punch in a numerical code to enter the main gate of the townhouse complex. There was a realtor's lockbox hanging from her front doorknob. David used his key in the main lock to enter and found that Maeva was not at home. Everything seemed to be the same as it was when he was last there. He checked his cell phone, and there were no messages from her. The only cellphone she ever had was her work phone. There was no way for him to contact her now. He left the townhouse and drove the twenty-five miles back to Elizabeth with a sick lonely feeling in the pit of his stomach. He hoped to find her Mazda in his driveway or garage but was disappointed. He sat with Grady on the back porch. The sky turned a bright orange on the mountainous western twilight horizon and then quickly went to total blackness.

CHAPTER 23

The next morning, David arose early and checked his cell phone. No messages. He made some coffee and let Grady out to roam his fenced two-acre backyard. David drank his coffee and glanced through his electronic version of the *Denver Post*. His mind wandered, and he had to reread several articles. He routinely read the comic section but could not concentrate that morning. He tried to exercise in his home gym but quickly found that he had no focus. He eventually gave up, showered, and drove to Maeva's townhouse. He couldn't think of anything else to do.

Wandering through her townhome, David noticed that most of Maeva's clothes and personal items had been removed. However, there was food in the refrigerator and a bottle of Grey Goose vodka in her freezer along with some frozen meat and vegetables. He looked at the clock on her microwave and noticed it was 1:00 p.m. He found an old-fashioned tumbler in her cabinet and poured two fingers of vodka into the glass. A cable news station was clicked on, and he sat on her living room loveseat with feet on her coffee table. Eventually, he dozed off.

David was awakened by the sound of the front door being opened. He startled upright and waited for Maeva to walk through the door. Instead there was an unknown woman who seemed as surprised as he was. The woman regained her composure instantly and approached him. "I am Karen Aubrey, the realtor representing this property. And you are?"

"David Richards. I am Maeva Sopo's friend. I'm trying to get in touch with her."

"Ah, yes. Ms. Sopo mentioned you and described you." Karen Aubrey was clearly evaluating how she should proceed. David noted that the woman was very professionally made-up and clothed. On closer inspection, she was probably twenty years older than she appeared. Her hair had been expertly colored and styled. Her figure was lean and taut. Perhaps she had benefited from Botox injections or had excellent genetics. Her face was unlined and smooth.

The realtor continued in a calm voice, "She said you would be coming to find her. When I saw that she had a healing black eye and redness this in the white of her left eye, I was afraid of what that meant. She assured me that you were her significant other and that you were trying to protect her. So I believe that you are who you say you are."

"I am just trying to find her and talk to her. She gave up her business cell phone. I believe it was her only cell phone."

"She gave up more than that. I know that she took her car over to AutoNation this morning and sold it. She took an Uber back to the townhouse. She put the townhome on the market yesterday, and I have four buyers at the present time. All four are willing to take the asking price, with the apartment completely furnished. The Denver market is a hot one. Few houses last more than a few days. A townhome in the Denver Technological Center is gold. As you know, this one has a view of the park and a second-story patio. It has security and much more charm than the apartments and condominiums that are being built today. I may be able to get her $20–$30,000 over the asking price. Maybe more if I can get the prospective buyers into a bidding war.

"I have a team of professional cleaners coming in this evening to toss the perishables and give it a finishing touch. Fortunately, your Maeva had a very Spartan lifestyle and the townhome will show well as is." Karen paused, realizing she was giving more of a sales pitch than information. "She had packed a large bag and was intent on walking over to the RTD light-rail train station when I convinced her to let me give her a lift. I believe her intent was to take the train all the way to Denver International Airport. I have a power of attorney to sell the property and forward the net proceeds to her."

"Can you tell me where she is going, and how I can get in touch with her?"

"First, would you mind showing me your driver's license and giving me Maeva's real full name? I am pretty sure you are who you say you are, but I am always hesitant to give personal information about a client." She smiled her wide professional smile.

David produced his identification and wrote Maeva's full, lengthy Polynesian surname on the back of one of his business cards.

The realtor nodded and said, "I am supposed to send the net sales proceeds, registered mail, to a general delivery post office on the island of Huahine Nui in French Polynesia. You probably know that Maeva is a resident alien in the USA. She still has a French passport and can travel back to her official domicile even as the international air travel is being restricted for tourists and foreigners by most governments. COVID-19 looks like it's going to bring international travel to a halt very soon. She seemed to want to get home while she still could. She also expects that you will find her."

*****

Thanksgiving was the next week. David was lonely and miserable. He had planned to spend the holiday watching football and lolling around the house with Grady. On the Tuesday of Thanksgiving week, Marc and Ruth Goodman called him and insisted that he join their family Thanksgiving celebration. Marc was insistent. David reluctantly agreed. David brought two bottles of Cabernet to the feast, and it was a fun, relaxing time.

"So when will you be traveling to Tahiti?" Marc inquired after his sons had vacated the table and Ruth had left the room while she started clearing dishes.

David took a sip of wine and said, "I will be looking to travel after the first of the year. The government promised that we are going to have vaccines very soon."

Unfortunately, the COVID-19 vaccines were not available to David until the springtime. He was not in one of the at-risk populations. He received two doses of the Pfizer vaccine, one in early March and one at the end of March. Once fully vaccinated and he had a medical card for proof, he started the red tape and documentation necessary to satisfy the French government for travel to their Polynesian Society Islands. Air passage was booked to Papeete, Tahiti, the capital of French Polynesia, for April.

He discovered that making arrangements for Grady to accompany him was considerably more difficult than providing his own medical documentation of immunization. He obtained a certified copy of all Grady's records of immunization and health. Grady was to be sealed in a crate until they arrived in Papeete. It was a long flight, but David could not arrange to have the big dog in the cabin with him despite his offer to purchase a human fare.

Four days before David was to depart, he received a call from Vic Beago. Marc Goodman had told Beago that David would be traveling to Huahine to find Maeva. Vic asked David if he could stop by the office to discuss some final details of Maeva's departure from the law firm. David agreed to meet that same afternoon.

Beago told David that Kingsley had made Maeva the beneficiary of his life insurance policy and stock ownership once his wife had passed away. There were no children to inherit. Kingsley's shares of stock could not be inherited by a nonlawyer, and there was an agreement that the life insurance proceeds would be used by the Kingsley law firm to purchase Kingsley's corporate shares from his estate. Kingsley's interest in the shares at his time of death translated into $500,000. That was the insurance policy that the law firm took out on the old lawyer. Beago had also discovered that Kingsley's personal life insurance policy also named Maeva as the beneficiary, following Mrs. Kingsley's death.

"When you see her, would you have her execute some documents, acknowledging receipt of the insurance proceeds? The insurance company isn't too keen on sending documents to a general delivery address. I told the company that you would be traveling to see her. You can transmit the checks and have her execute the accompanying documentation before a notary or whatever type of French official can formally acknowledge the transfer. They have offered to pay you for your time."

"That will not be necessary. I'll take the checks and the accompanying documentation with me and arrange the transfer. That is, if she is where I expect her to be."

"Send her the firm's best wishes. Please tell her that I hope to see her again sometime. When the time is right, of course."

David realized that Beago and his fellow minority shareholder, Ms. Brown, would soon be the sole shareholders of Kingsley, Beago, and Brown, P. C. Their loyalty to the law firm would be handsomely rewarded. They would have controlling interest in an established law firm with a solid clientele. David was sure that Maeva would have no reason to anticipate her windfall. He accepted the checks and documentation along with a stamped and self-addressed envelope to the law firm.

CHAPTER 24

On their departure date, David waited and walked Grady until the airline insisted on loading him into the airplane's freight hold. The freight handler promised David that he had taken care of many pets on flights and would make sure that Grady had water. David still felt guilty about the situation and gave the airline representative two $20 bills for his trouble.

David hurried back to the terminal. He had purchased a first-class ticket so that his 6'4" frame could be relatively comfortable during the long flight. His size and moderate claustrophobia made air travel difficult under the best of circumstances. After takeoff and a tolerable luncheon plate, he swallowed a tranquilizer with a can of German beer. He fell asleep during an animated Disney movie. David woke up in time for a fruit and cheese plate with buttery club crackers. After another German beer, he started watching a wildlife documentary until he fell asleep again.

He awakened when the pilot announced that they would soon be starting their descent into the French Polynesian capital and that all passengers needed to fill out immigration forms which would be collected by the flight attendants before arrival.

The sight of emerald-green forest-clad peaks and crystal-clear blue ocean excited David as they descended toward the French Polynesia capital. He had read about Papeete and its infusions of Tahitian, French, and Chinese culture. The pilot told the passengers to look toward the island of Mo'orea in the distance. Clouds covered the tops of the distant volcanic peaks. Despite the natural beauty below him, David felt a nervous knot in his stomach about seeing Maeva again. It had been over five months, and he had not spoken to her during that time. He had started to write several letters to send to the general delivery address the realtor had given him but could never find the right words to say. Now he wished that he had sent something.

David hurried through customs and rescued Grady from his travel crate before collecting his luggage. The climate was warm that day but not too humid. He parked his luggage by a taxi stand and tipped an attendant to watch his bags while he gave Grady a long walk near the airport grounds. When he returned, the attendant found a taxi that would accept a large dog. They headed off to his lodging, which was a collection of grass-thatched bungalows near the ocean. All this was arranged even though David spoke very little French and the Tahitians at the airport spoke very little English.

Papeete was a bustling island port town. Traffic was fairly light at midday. The cab driver pulled into the hotel grounds and assisted David with the luggage. A thin sandy-haired and bearded man in his late thirties, clad in khaki cargo shorts and a T-shirt, emerged from the office and greeted them. He spoke English and appeared to be either American or Canadian. He said his name was John Delaney and that he was the manager of the hotel.

He took David's large suitcase on wheels and showed his new lodger to one of the thatched huts. Delaney was friendly and seemed eager to converse in English. The hotel manager said that he was from Boston and said that he had always wanted to travel to Colorado when David introduced himself. He left and returned with a bowl for Grady's water. Delaney volunteered that he had visited Tahiti and Mo'orea when he was in his early twenties, fell in love with the islands, and had been in French Polynesia ever since. It had been long enough to learn both French and Tahitian.

He gave David directions to the nearest Chinese market, the Tahitian version of a general store, and several inexpensive restaurants. Most of the restaurants had outside tables and would accommodate a dog.

David was eager to stretch his legs and take Grady for a long walk. They walked past the Chinese store and walked along the roadway for at least two miles. Grady seemed excited by the new smells of Tahiti but made sure to walk close to David for a sense of security in a new world.

When they saw the Chinese store again, David started to enter. There was an Asian woman at an old-fashioned cash register at a table near the entrance. David gestured toward his dog, and the woman shook her head as if to indicate that it was permissible for the dog to enter the store. David purchased two ham-and-cheese sandwiches on baguettes with tomato and lettuce. He also bought two pint cans of Hinano beer. He carried them back to his lodging in a large plastic bag. He also bought some French kibble and canned fish for Grady.

Delaney was raking around the huts when David returned. David showed him the sandwiches and beers. Delaney ushered them over to a picnic table. Delaney walked over to the manager's office and returned with two large unpeeled citron fruits. David was unfamiliar with the fruit and watched as Delaney peeled away the thick fleshy rind to reveal a round core that resembled a peeled grapefruit. In fact, the citrus fruit had the harsh citrus tang of a grapefruit. They ate their sandwiches and drank the beer. Delaney found a bowl so that David could mix the dog kibble and canned fish for Grady.

When they had finished their meal, Delaney asked: "What brings you to French Polynesia, brother? It is not every tourist who brings a dog with them."

"My girl lives in Huahine. She left the States before the pandemic shut down tourist travel. She would expect Grady to be with me. They have grown quite close. I need to travel to Huahine as soon as I can. Do you know where I could hire a boat to take us both over to that island?"

"There are planes every day from Papeete to Huahine. No need to go by boat."

"I feel like I have traumatized Grady too much already. I think he would be better off on a boat. He has been on fishing boats before and seemed to be comfortable. Another airplane ride just doesn't seem right."

"Suit yourself. I know a lot of guys who would jump at the opportunity to sail you over to Huahine for a reasonable price. It will be a nice trip. Let's go over to the Island Gem Bar at 5:00 p.m. If you're buying the beer, I will introduce you to some reputable sailors. Bring Grady too so there's no mystery about his temperament."

*****

David knocked on the manager's door before 5:00 p.m. Delaney led them to the bar which was only three or four blocks away. The sign at the entrance was in French. It had a thatched palm roof and tile floor. The Island Gem Bar was open-aired on two walls. The smell of sea breeze mixed with the faint traces of city exhaust fumes and fish frying. Grady was once again welcomed. They found a card table with four folding chairs. After ordering beers, they waited patiently and enjoyed the ambience.

When they had finished the first round, David walked up to the bar for seconds. A pretty native waitress with an apron approached him, smiled, and bounced her hip off of his. She said something in French and waved David away from the bar. David shrugged and shook his head to indicate he could not understand her. She said, "I bring to table. Go sit down."

Delaney was chuckling to himself when David returned. The waitress followed him and set down the beers at their table. She beamed at David. Delaney said, "That hip bounce from our waitress, Nicole by the way, is the method by which some Tahitian women let you know that they appreciate your good looks and would like to get to know you. I feel fairly certain that you may encounter that island greeting again."

Delaney appeared to be well known at the Island Gem Bar. When other patrons entered, they addressed him in Tahitian, French, or English. He seemed comfortable conversing in any of the three languages. When two young burly tattooed native men came in, Delaney motioned them over to their card table. He said something in French and motioned for Nicole to bring four more beers to their table.

Delaney introduced the new arrivals to David as Martin and Tua. He said that they were fishermen and owned their own boat. He alternated between French and English depending on who he was addressing. He told Martin that David was looking to travel to Huahine with his dog. Martin reached down and scratched Grady on the muzzle.

Martin seemed eager to try out his sparse English. He looked at David and said, "I can sail to Huahine in two days." He held up two fingers to emphasize his words. "I must fish tomorrow." Martin turned to both Tua and Delaney to speak French. He explained the cost of the trip, the time and place of departure, and then waited for Delaney to translate the details in English. Martin followed along with Delaney and moved his lips. He understood more English than he could speak.

David nodded his agreement and raised his beer to toast their arrangement. Everyone smiled and drank deeply.

CHAPTER 25

Maeva had just returned from Mata'irea Hill, where she had visited the ancient archaeological sites. Over the last few months she had frequently walked from her rented cottage to the ruins for exercise and peace of mind. Given her new circumstances, she was content to replace exercise equipment and running with walking up and down island roads and paths.

Huahine Nui, the larger of the two Huahine islands separated by a blue bay and ringed by a coral atoll, was where she had been born and mostly raised. Her aunt, nieces, and nephews lived nearby. Her mother had passed away before she had traveled to the States. They were a close family, and all her relatives welcomed her return with warmth and affection. She was required to talk about her travel and adventures outside of French Polynesia on an almost daily basis.

As she neared her cottage, a thin feral gray cat started to follow her. She had been feeding this cat with scraps from her meals, and the cat seemed to have adopted her. She stooped and cradled the small cat in her arm as she walked down the road. The island was as lush and green as she had remembered it. The foliage and the soil made the air rich and sweet in her nostrils. It was a restful tropical setting. It was also home.

Maeva had neither a telephone nor a television in the rented cottage. Whatever news from the outside world reached her, it was either from a local French language radio station or was filtered through neighbors or relatives. She had recently heard that the pandemic ban on tourism and air travel to French Polynesia had been lifted by the French government for those who could prove that they were fully vaccinated against COVID-19. Tourism was an important part of the local economy, and most Huahine residents saw the return of travelers as a good thing.

Maeva was both excited and nervous. Each day and night, she imagined her reunion with David. He would be vaccinated as soon as he could. What would he think of her new circumstances? Should she have written to him to explain? Would he be content to stay with her on the island for a while? Would he want to go back to Colorado? She longed to know what he was thinking even as she was unsure about her own future.

Of course, she could never go back to her prior life. Killing a coworker, even an attempted rapist, had changed everything. But what about David? He had seemed ready to transition into some sort of retirement. What would that look like? He might be too young to retire and want to go back to his law practice. How would she fit in to his plans? Could he accept her new circumstances? Would they feel the same about each other? She wanted to know but was afraid to find out.

Maeva was hungry when she got back to her cottage. She had a fresh fish fillet in her refrigerator, which she put in a pan with some oil and herbs. She chopped up mangoes, citron, and bananas for a fruit salad. She poured a cup of drinking water from a plastic jug. When the fish was fried, she sat out on her front porch and shared it with her cat friend. They sat together and watched the sun go down through the palm fronds.

CHAPTER 26

The three men and a dog set sail for Huahine at the respectable hour of eight o'clock on the scheduled morning. The sky was cloudless, and the ocean was pale blue. The fishing boat had a glass bottom. As they passed over coral reefs, they could see eels, barracuda, and other large tropical fish. Large rays were common and could be seen right below the surface of the sea. Grady jumped up on the prow of the boat behind some ornamental railings. David was nervous, but Tua and Martin waved their hands to indicate that everything was okay.

Grady seemed happy to have the sea air blowing through his curly hair and bask in the Tahitian sun. David was glad that he had not subjected Grady to another airline flight, whether crammed in the baggage compartment or on the floor of the passenger area. It certainly wouldn't have been as picturesque and calming as the boat ride. Grady soon put his head down and closed his eyes, enjoying the purring of the boat motor.

It wasn't long before they sailed near Mo'orea. Martin said, "*Bali Hai*," and pointed to the ancient volcanic peaks covered in low clouds. David understood the reference to the South Pacific musical.

He wondered if it actually been filmed on that gorgeous island. He could see houses painted in pastel hues on the shoreline. The hills were covered with lush greenery. He wanted to find a way to come back to this island and explore. However, his heart beat fast when thinking of how soon he would be on Maeva's island.

Grady eventually sought out some shade under the fishing boat's canvas roof. He glanced at the submerged terrain below the glass bottom of the boat but did not seem to understand the reality of what was passing below him. It was similar to when he was looking at David's television screen and presumably seeing moving shapes and indistinct sounds.

As they were passing over a reef on the far side of Mo'orea, Tua suddenly cut the engine and pointed out over the port bow. Martin asked David if he had a camera. David pulled out his cell phone. Martin nodded, pulled his T-shirt over his head, and picked up a spear gun from a side pocket in the boat. He gestured toward the glass bottom of the boat and then dived overboard.

David watched as Martin speared a fish off the reef. He then disappeared for a moment and then returned swimming under the glass bottom with the speared fish still wriggling. An eight-foot-long whitetip reef shark was following the wriggling and bleeding fish on the end of Martin's spear. Martin placed the struggling fish against the glass bottom of the boat. The shark came up to the glass, opened its toothy mouth and took the fish off the spear.

Fortunately, David was ready and got several pictures of the shark taking the prey. Grady even barked when the shark was just below the glass bottom. Tua and David laughed. Martin climbed over the side of the boat and gave a big thumbs-up to David. David raised his phone and returned the thumbs-up sign. He showed the photos to Martin, who appreciated the clarity of the images shot through the glass bottom of the boat.

"Aren't you afraid that the shark will bite you?" David asked.

"No. The shark don't care about me when there's a bleeding fish for his meal." Martin laughed. "You watch too many movies and TV."

David dozed in the sun for a while in one of the fishing chairs facing the stern of the boat. He was awakened by someone shaking his shoulder.

Tua pointed out in the distance. He said, "Huahine." David looked and saw what appeared to be two islands separated by a deep blue bay and surrounded by a coral atoll. Martin stood up, nodded, and handed David a pair of binoculars. He said, "Maeva."

David looked at him with surprise and said, "What did you say?"

"Famous town on Huahine. Maeva. Is that where you will go?"

"I am actually looking for a woman named Maeva who lives here. I am not sure exactly where."

Martin nodded and said, "Many girls and women have the Maeva name in the Society Islands. You may be searching."

The boat pulled up to a wooden pier. Tua tossed rope lines to a thin native teenaged boy who rushed out to meet the boat. The boy fastened the lines to the pier. He watched Martin, Tua, and David climb out of the boat. When Grady jumped up to follow them, the boy quickly retreated.

"He may bark, but he's not going to bite. He's a friendly dog," David said reassuringly, as Grady put his head down and approached the unknown teenager. Martin translated in French. Grady sniffed the teenager and started wagging his tail. The young man tentatively reached out to the dog with an unopened hand. Grady sniffed him again and then allowed his head to be patted between his ears.

Martin spoke to the teenager in French at first and then in Tahitian. He eventually turned to David and said, "This boy is called Tai. Maybe he can help you find your woman, Maeva."

David addressed the boy directly: "No French. No Tahitian. I am looking for a woman named Maeva who came from the United States a few months ago." The teenager listened but obviously did not understand. David paused and then pronounced Maeva's actual Polynesian surname the way she had taught him with the correct cadence and accent. "Sometimes she calls herself Maeva Sopo."

Tai beamed widely and nodded. "*Tante* Maeva." He said something else in Tahitian to Martin and Tua.

111

"The boy says that the woman is his *tante,* his auntie. He says that you are the husband she waits for. He wants you to follow him."

Tua handed David his large sea bag and backpack from the fishing boat. Tai dragged the heavy seabag over to a wooden hut at the end of the pier and pointed to an older Caucasian man sitting behind a wooden bar. Tai made a drinking motion with his hand. The old man pulled up three bottles of Hinano beer and a Coca-Cola. He used a bottle opener on each and set them on the bar. David passed them around and then addressed the bartender, "Do you speak English?"

The bartender had stark white hair and the deepwater tan of a fisherman. He said, in a thick French accent, "I must speak English to deal with tourists who rent fishing boats and gear. I also know a few Japanese sayings. Can I help you with something?"

"I'm looking for a native woman by the name of Maeva who traveled here recently from America. This boy says that she may be his aunt." David pronounced her surname again with the correct Tahitian accent. Tai excitedly nodded his head again and spoke to the old man in French.

"This woman did move here a few months ago, and she is his relative. She lives in a house approximately five kilometers from here. You and Tai may use two of my tourist bicycles to travel there. Very few are being rented this time of the year. It's too late to catch a ride with the postman or the bakery deliveryman. I can have one of them drop your heavy bag when they travel the routes tomorrow in the morning."

Apparently, almost every Huahine home had a mailbox and a second slender box that would accept fresh loaves of paper-wrapped baguettes. It was important to have fresh daily bread on a French island even if that island was thousands of miles away from France in the southern Pacific Ocean. The juxtaposition of tropical wild with European civilization amused David.

David paid Martin and Tua for the voyage and bought them another round of Hinano beers. He was in a hurry to travel the 5 km and see Maeva for the first time in months. The old white-haired man, who eventually introduced himself as Jacques, dragged David's seabag behind his bar and assured David that it would be safe over-night. Tai wheeled over two rusty fat-tired bikes with baskets below the front handlebars. David noted that they were girl's bicycles but said nothing.

Jacques held up his hand for David and Tai to wait while the old man adjusted David's seat and handlebars with a wrench to accom-modate the American's height. When finished, he raised his hands and said, "Voila. Bring the bikes back in the next week." He repeated the words to Tai in French. He also said, in French for Tai's benefit, "Don't stay too long with your auntie. They will need time alone. Husband and wife time."

Tai laughed a knowing laugh and nodded his head to Jacques. He started pedaling his way down a one-laned dirt road lined with overhead electrical lines on wooden poles. David put on his back-pack and clumsily followed on the old single-speed bicycle. Grady kept pace behind them.

They traveled between dense foliage, thick with banana trees and coconut palms. Birds, chickens, feral cats, and pigs would scatter from the roadway when the riders passed through. Grady would stop to bark briefly. He wanted to keep pace with Tai and David. When Tai noticed that David was lagging, he would slow his speed and allow David and Grady to catch up.

CHAPTER 27

The trio followed a right-hand turn in the dirt roadway. A small thatch-roofed house stood in the middle of a field. Tai rode his bicycle across the field and parked it with its kickstand in front of the door. Grady blazed past some chickens, paused next to Tai, and then hurried through the front door of the house. The next sound was a woman's scream, a happy scream, and the word, "Grady." David let his bicycle fall next to Tai's and walked through the open door.

Maeva was on her knees with her arms around Grady's neck. She wore a long red cotton dress with large white flowers. Grady was licking her face, wagging his tail, and whining.

"There you are," David said from the threshold. "May I come in too?"

Maeva slowly rose to her feet. When she reached her full height, the red cotton dress clung to her front. She was visibly pregnant, very pregnant. She put her hands on the baby bump and leaned back to tentatively, and then proudly, display her condition. David hurried to embrace her. They kissed, cried briefly, laughed, and kissed again.

Grady was circling them, still whining. Tai stood at the threshold, watching the reunion with amusement.

Maeva said, "Bye-bye, Tai. *Merci*." Tai responded with a thumbs-up gesture, mounted his bicycle, and rode away.

They continued their embrace, kissing and laughing. Eventually, David said, "Is Tai really your nephew? That seems like quite a coincidence."

"His mother is a distant cousin of mine. My midwife actually. It's not unusual for youngsters to refer to any adult female relative who is not part of the immediate family circle as *tante*. He is a sweet kid."

David put his arm around Maeva and held her closely as he walked toward the open door. He gazed at the tropical fruits and flowers that lined her grassy field and listened to the sound of the birds chattering in the late afternoon. "This is magnificent. It's really paradise. How could you ever leave here?"

Maeva put her palms on his chest and pressed her baby bump into his midsection. "If you'd asked me that question a year ago, I would have confidentially given you all the logical reasons I needed to find my way in the outside world."

As they were embracing and staring out the open door, a large sow and four pink and black piglets came roaming down the road and started to cut across the field surrounding Maeva's house. Grady ran up to them and started barking territorially. The sow and the piglets turned and trotted away toward whence they had come.

Grady proudly walked in through the door, and Maeva shut it behind him. "So what took you guys so long to find me? For months I have walked every inch of this island, explored every historical archaeological site, and watched endless ocean waves crash against the reefs."

"Only a worldwide travel ban, a raging COVID-19 pandemic, and the lack of universally available vaccines," David said with a deadpan tone. He kissed her deeply again.

"Good thing I didn't move to Mo'orea already. I found a fabulous old French house and a small mango plantation last month. There's an older couple who want to rent it or sell it to a native. I want to show it to you. It's got a walled garden so that Grady and the baby won't wander away."

David looked around at Maeva's dwelling. It had a thatched roof and an open-air gap between the roof and the walls. This was a common design in French Polynesia. The cottage had an open floor plan with a combined living room, dining area, and kitchen with a separate bedroom and bathroom. He said, "You haven't given me much time to get used to your current digs. However, I think we will be able to afford the property in Mo'orea even if we have to buy it rather than rent it. Old Kingsley made you the beneficiary of his company stock and insurance policies. Also—" He was about to tell her that he had hired her Colorado realtor, Karen, and had given Marc Goodman a power of attorney to sell the Elizabeth property. All they were waiting for was his call.

Maeva interrupted him and put a hand over his mouth. "You lawyers always want to talk too much. All I care about is that you and Grady are here, finally. We can talk about the future when we are done enjoying the present." Maeva rubbed against him and rested her head on his chest. She said, in an uncertain tone, "You have not said one word about the baby. I have worried every day about what your reaction might be."

David placed both hands on her swollen belly and kissed her repeatedly on her full lips. "That must be why the locals are referring to me as 'the husband.' Actually, I have been thinking about how to work around that baby bump."

Maeva smiled enigmatically. She led him by the hand through the curtained wall to her bedroom. She removed his travel clothes and pushed him onto her double bed. She pulled the flowered dress over her head, revealing the athletic figure that he knew so well. She straddled him on the bed and placed him inside her. They both soon discovered that the baby bump was not an issue.

"You seem to have found the right place, mister," Maeva moaned. "I knew you would."

ABOUT THE AUTHOR

Mark lives in Elbert County, Colorado, with his wife, Lynn, two dogs (sometimes three), and two parrots. They have lived there since 2011.

Mark was raised and worked in Metropolitan Denver, Colorado. He received his high school diploma from Thomas Jefferson High School in Denver, Colorado. He received his bachelor of arts degree from the University of Colorado at Boulder. He received his Juris Doctor from the University of San Diego in California.

Mark was a trial attorney practicing all over the state of Colorado. The majority of his professional work was defending injury cases. He occasionally represented plaintiffs or claimants in injury cases.